ONCE UPON A TIME IN THE SIXTIES

9-4-13

To Chris

ONCE UPON A TIME IN THE SIXTIES

By

PETER MADDICK

With love

Peter Maddick

Bookline & Thinker Ltd
London

Bookline & Thinker Ltd
#231, 405 King's Road
London SW10 0BB
Tel: 0845 116 1476
www.booklinethinker.com

A CIP catalogue for this book is available from the British Library.

ISBN: 9780956847669

Cover design by Donald McColl
Printed and bound by Lightning Source UK

For Caroline, Emily and Barnaby

"The thing the sixties did was to show us the possibilities and the responsibility that we all had. It wasn't the answer. It just gave us a glimpse of the possibility."

John Lennon

Once upon a time in the sixties...

According to my "ticka-tick" Timex watch it's a little after 9am. I'm in a building at St James's Square, London. The address is posh, and the names on the office doors include three double-barrels and, believe it or not, a triple-barrel. This is my first proper job and I'm nervously hoping I don't bump into any of those names. They are ad men and as smooth as Roger Moore in *The Saint*. At least that's what I've been told.

So far I haven't seen a soul. Yet there's life somewhere as I can hear the click-click-click of a typewriter or two. I can also hear someone running, clattering along the linoleum floor in what must be leather-soled shoes with steel-caps, the kind ex-army people wear in homage to their old parade ground. I hear a grunt, a curse. Clearly the person is being chased and should be stopped. I stand around the bend, where I can't be seen, my arms spread open. Wham! I'm flat on my face staring at a pair of highly polished black lace-up shoes, just the kind that would have steel–caps.

I see long burgundy socks leading up to a pair of gentlemen's suspenders, and knees like rock cakes hovering below boxer shorts with vintage cars on them.

The man bawls at me, "Have you seen my secretary?"

I lift myself up without a helping hand.

Apart from the missing trousers he's immaculately turned out in a blue and white striped shirt with a stiff white detachable collar, red and white polka dot tie, and immaculately groomed jet-black Brylcreemed hair.

"The wretched gal has gorn 'orff with m' trousers again. All I asked her to do was press them!" He shouts in disbelief.

I gulp and apologize for not having seen her, not that I'd know her if I fell across her.

"Well you're no bloody good!"

He pushes me to one side and races off down the corridor, shirttails flapping like a character in a Brian Rix farce, where trousers are regularly dropped to get a laugh. But I'm not laughing. I feel like running for it, straight to the lifts, down to the main entrance, passed the commissionaire and out the front door.

ONE

LONDON

Mid October 1963

"CAN I HELP YOU... *SIR*?"

I've never been called "sir" before. Not sure I want to be, particularly when I'm being shouted at by a commissionaire in a pseudo-army uniform.

"I have a 2.30 interview with Major Millard." I explain and am ordered to take the lift to the fifth floor reception.

It's eerily quiet when I get out of the elevator. I take a deep breath, feeling suddenly aware of my new C&A suit. The one my father insisted I'd grow into though it makes me feel like a cross between a refugee and a clown, especially outdoors when the wind blows and the jacket billows. I was a perfectly happy sixteen-year-old school leaver, leading a beatnik-inspired existence listening to R&B performed by my favourite new group, Mick and the Blue Boys, at the Ealing Jazz Club.

My parents, however, had other ideas. A golfing pal of my father said that his advertising company were recruiting trainees.

I tentatively push the glass doors and enter a large reception area. Three sides have floor-to-ceiling shelves that display well-known household products – Weetabix, Mars, Colgate, Mobil Oil, Wilkinson Sword. Two women sit behind a long wooden desk. One is middle-aged with heavy white make-up and mascara. A prominently hooked nose gives her a haughty air, making me think of the eccentric poet Dame Edith Sitwell. The other woman is much younger and looks as if she's stepped out of the *Debutante of the month* page in *Tatler* – a perfect serene brunette in twin-set and pearls.

"Do take a seat," the brunette says. She has a particularly husky, velvety voice, like the breathy actress Fenella Fielding. "Major Millard's secretary will fetch you in just a few minutes."

She gives me a smile showing just a hint of immaculate white teeth. The haughty woman ignores me.

My eyes settle on some miniature bottles of Babycham, one of my mother's favourite tipples. The husky purr strikes up again.

"The managing director of the agency invented that product. The client was so delighted with the sales they presented him with a personalized Rolls Royce. Wasn't that kind?"

Before I can reply a stout girl with a ruddy complexion and frumpy clothes hurries in. She races me along a deserted corridor as if we are late for an important date. I ask why it's so quiet.

The secretary clears her throat as if to make an important announcement. "This is the fifth floor, the director's floor. It's generally quiet here, particularly at this time of day." She gives a knowing smile and whispers, "Luncheon!"

At the far end of the corridor we pause before a white wooden door. The secretary adopts her conspiratorial tone again. "You'll love the major. He's a real sweetie."

She cautiously opens the door.

Without bothering to look up Major Millard gestures for me to sit. My heart thumps like a sledgehammer. The personnel director couldn't be anything other than a retired army man: a plump well-fed face, slicked-back silver hair, a nose just a touch too purple and, beneath it, a small twitchy moustache. He studies the papers before him. After a few minutes he fixes me with a steely gaze and bellows.

"So you've come to apologize have you?" He slams his hand on the desk. "What do you have to say for yourself, eh?"

I manage to croak out my name adding, "trainee job."

He looks angrily confused. "So where the blazes is Mulligan then?"

The secretary appears and hands her boss what must be my job application. He flicks through the form and grunts. "Are you sure you want to work in advertising?"

I nod but would love to give the honest answer.

"And what part of the business interests you most?"

My basic homework has come up with an astonishing conclusion: that advertising is all about pictures and words, very often not many words at all. Given the choice I'd really like to go for the pictures side particularly as I fancy so many of the girls shown in the ads. The problem is that I'm not very good at art.

I mumble about wanting to write advertisements.

Suddenly the major turns even more purple. He slams his fist on his desk for a second time. "Are you mad, boy?"

He waves my job application at me. "Dreadful types the creative lot! Just look at that Mulligan fellow. Molests a girl in the lift and he hasn't even got the courage to come and face up to me. Irish I believe, like that Oscar Wilde deviant. You're not Irish are you?"

Without having time to answer the question, not that I think it needs one, the jolly-hockey-stick secretary rescues me.

"So that seems to have gone well," she says. "I told you he was an old sweetie."

She also tells me that I'll receive a letter from the major within the next few days.

I don't talk much to my parents about the interview. To be honest, I wouldn't really know where to begin. Instead, I lock myself in my room listening to Miles Davis' *Kind of Blue* while drafting a letter to Mick asking if there is any chance of joining the group as a roadie.

Dear Mick, you may not remember me but I'm the bloke who bought you a few beers at Ealing Jazz Club when you were skint. Now that you and the lads are a bit more famous and that, and I do think Come On *is a cool single and should stuff the Beatles, I was wondering…*

Unfortunately a short letter arrives from the major a couple of days later offering me a position as a trainee on a starting salary of £6 per week with luncheon vouchers. I'm told to report at 8.30am the following Monday. My parents are delighted. The Rolling Stones will have to live without me.

TWO

This time I manage to slip past the commissionaire while he's bawling-out a messenger boy. I confidently stroll over to join a group waiting for a lift: a well-dressed woman, a scruffy bearded man in a duffle coat and two other men in overcoats, one in a bowler hat casually reading *The Times*. Nobody speaks. For a moment I wonder if I should introduce myself. The wood-panelled lift arrives and I press the button for the fifth floor. Everyone gets off on the lower floors, which is a relief. I'm looking forward to seeing the brunette receptionist again. I wonder what her name is – probably something smart like Antoinette or perhaps Amanda.

The haughty older lady is alone. I explain that I have to report to Mr. Smaile…Mr. Stanley Smaile.

She looks at me as if I'd just arrived from a dustbin. "You're in the wrong place. You need the side entrance on Charles II Street."

She wafts her arms across the desk, presumably in case some filth has fallen from me. The phone saves further humiliation and she answers with a syrupy voice while gesticulating that I should leave immediately.

Things are a bit different on Charles II Street. A double-door entrance is wedged open to allow passage of a large trolley laden with corrugated rolls of paper. The doorway leads onto a ramp and into an untidy basement.

A man in a long brown workman's smock asks, "Ere! What you after, then?"

My white shirt, tie and the absurd three-piece navy blue suit has clearly confused him. Luckily I'm not sent straight back to the main reception, but I do feel like a tailors' dummy moving around a gents outfitters until a suitable display area is found. After a shifty look he points me in the direction of Mr. Smaile's office.

I make my way through a long dingy corridor with stained linoleum floor. Strips of neon light make it impossible to tell between day and night. Through glass partitioning, I see storage areas full of unmarked boxes, piles of metal film canisters and other random objects in shadowy recesses. There's a faint buzz from what could be a generator. I'm reminded of war films depicting submarine claustrophobia – *The Enemy Below*. I wonder if there's been a mistake. The smart brunette wouldn't have sent me to the basement.

As a cardboard box comes flying from a doorway, a voice calls out. "Keep the racket down lads!"

There seems to be a fight going on, but I step into the first doorway. "Sorry to trouble you, I've been told to report here."

Without taking any notice of me, Mr. Smaile, and I have to assume that this is *the* Mr. Smaile I've come to work for, gets up from behind his desk, walks into the corridor, picks up the cardboard box and throws it back into the unseen room. He is a short, stocky man with cherry-red cheeks and large eyes like a ventriloquist's dummy. He hardly opens his mouth as he welcomes me to dispatch.

I point out that I'm a trainee.

"So are the other five lads sitting next door," he replies.

The room next door is large with no windows, just sharp neon lighting. Six wooden chairs, like school chairs, line one wall. Opposite are four worn, mismatched armchairs. A custom-built packing table runs along the far end. Five young men of about my age are seated on the school chairs, all dressed in collar and tie; some in suits, others in sports jacket and flannels.

Seated opposite are three older men in identical navy blue serge suits, a touch too similar to mine for comfort. A tubby man of indiscernible age jerks about in the middle of the room, as if suffering from a fit of St Vitus' Dance. He appears to be in great distress and is shouting obscenities at random. Empty cardboard boxes litter the floor. One of the three older men picks up a box and hurls it at the dancing man. He twitches around to face the young lads thinking it's one of them. As he struggles to shout an obscenity, they cringe as if he's about to set about them. While this is happening one of the older men creeps up behind him and grabs his arse.

"Get your ffffuckkin hhhhand of my sssodding arse you fffilthy fffucking queer." The dancing man is purple in the face and slightly foaming at the mouth. He turns on the arse-grabber and chases him out the room, almost knocking me over as they pass. The remaining teasers cheer. One puts two fingers to his mouth and lets out a high-pitched whistle. A sinister-looking character with a pockmarked face and the worst toupee imaginable ignores it all and sits behind the packing desk at the far end of the room picking his fingernails with a Stanley knife.

Mr. Smaile makes another appearance. "I said, keep the bloody racket down!"

It's my own fault. I should have asked more questions at the interview. I vaguely remember the major mumbling that the trainee scheme was a way to learn the different departments in a large advertising agency, but at that stage I thought only of getting out of the interview alive. The bridge between trainee and post boy is slowing sinking in. The other lads greet me like a new prisoner entering the dungeon.

Mr. Smaile appears again in the doorway and shouts, "Okay lads, get to it!"

The five dispatch boys shuffle off to another room. One is instructed to show me the ropes; I've been given the sixth floor. A bank of open pigeon-holes is numbered 1-6 with a typed list of the people on the floor. The morning mail has already been allocated to its slot together with items not delivered the previous night. I'm instructed to deliver the mail first, which means sorting it into the correct order. Then I must reverse the procedure and collect anything put in the out-tray and bring it back to the basement. Not exactly challenging once you've got the hang of it!

The delivery and collection process happens three times each morning and the same again in the afternoon. In between, there are ad hoc deliveries of newspapers, magazines and special packages to the floors. The rules are straightforward: don't speak to anyone unless they speak to you, only deal with secretaries, never, but never, disturb or talk to an account director. My floor has a mixture of senior account executives and group directors – whatever they are.

And so on my first morning, I set off to deliver my mail only to be flattened by a rising star, a 'suit' without any trousers on.

THREE

It's Friday evening November 22, a week after my 17th birthday. The girl I'm currently seeing has come round and we're sitting in my bedroom listening to a newly released LP. Her dad owns a department store and gets all the new releases on the day. They are pretty rich and have a big house about a mile away, one with a drive.

We're not really that keen on the Beatles but it's the LP cover that has caught her eye – a cool, moody shot of the group in shadow. She's a student at Harrow School of Art. That's why she likes to sit topless in my room, all to do with life drawing and freedom of expression. The problem is, I'm not allowed to touch. Normally she's reading aloud a poem by Lawrence Ferlighetti, her favourite. Sometimes reading Alan Ginsberg seems to get her hand roaming towards my trousers. I always leave a slim paperback of his beat poems lying about just in case. This time she's sitting naked from the waist up, her boyish figure swaying to *You Really Got a Hold on Me*.

Suddenly there's a frantic knocking on the door and my father is yelling, "Come downstairs immediately. Something terrible has happened."

Our Radio Rentals black and white TV set is showing that the President of the United States of America has been shot dead. A couple of weeks ago we were watching the Beatles in their silly little suits on *Sunday Night at the London Palladium*, hearing about their plans to tour America. Now our small television screen is full of the off-focus horror of assassination – all from the land that gave us bubblegum, Coca Cola and Rhythm and Blues.

The funny thing is, not that it's really funny at all, I mention the JFK tragedy at work, and the MD's chauffeur doubles-up with laughter. He's the one who drives the personalized Roller, who appears to laugh at everything and everybody. He's like one of those automatons I remember from seaside piers, put a penny in the slot and he'll laugh his head off at you. It's just as well the MD's not one for cracking jokes, otherwise the car would be written off before they got out of St James's Square.

The other two chauffeurs are basic cowardly bullies, particularly the arse-grabber who learned his manners on the terraces at White Hart Lane.

The other one bangs on about sissy boys, implying that anyone who "talks proper" has to be one. And as for poor Chester, the outside messenger with a stutter and a lisp who foams at the mouth when provoked, well according to the chauffeur, he's most definitely "one of them".

The dispatch lads are a mixed bunch too: an aspiring playboy who uses the office phone to chat up girlfriends by saying he lives in St James's Square; a Jewish wannabe showbiz star who does an irritating impersonation of Sammy Davis Jnr tap-dancing; an aloof guy who never speaks and brings in a mini-hamper lunch each day; a rather dull nerd who reads Sci-Fi magazines; a clumsy rugger-bugger; and me. The sissy-hating chauffeur has picked up on the fact that I lived in Australia as a youngster, which somehow gives me a macho edge despite my seemingly "posh" accent. I play on it, particularly the sea voyage home through the Suez Canal; you know, stowaways eaten by sharks, that kind of half-truth. He's nicknamed me Ned, as in Kelly.

"Ere lad. Go out and see if you can find Chester will you?" This is a fairly regular occurrence - the poor tormented foot messenger often gets lost.

"I sent him up to Soho Square over an hour ago. God knows where he's got to."

I put on my donkey jacket as it's cold outside. It's good to get out of the dungeon. I walk up Lower Regent Street to Piccadilly Circus with Lillywhites on the corner. I notice in the window a poster announcing that the England cricket legend and Brylcreem boy, Denis Compton, will be making a guest appearance. I walk on past Swan and Edgar with their tinselled Christmas decorations in the windows and along Brewer Street where I smirk at hand-written notes next to a scruffy doorbell announcing *French lessons given,* and cross Wardour Street to Old Compton Street where I take a quick look in the window of Del Monaco's at all the imported wines and spirits with labels showing matadors, and Greek dancers before heading up Dean Street to Soho Square.

I love Soho, a bohemian village in the heart of London. I don't know it very well. I've visited the Marquee a few times in Wardour Street, once to see Mick and the lads, the other time to hear a new group, Manfred Mann, who have taken over Mick's Ealing Jazz Club slot.

I arrive at the address Chester was sent to and find he has left. I wander into the garden square with its twee cottage pavilion and there see our foot messenger, sitting on a bench feeding pigeons with bread-crumbs from a paper bag. He looks lonely and sad. Removed from the turmoil of dispatch, his strange egg-like shape is more prominent. I feel sorry for him living a life of constant teasing and abuse. He looks like Humpty Dumpty about to fall.

I approach slowly not wanting to disturb the birds and quietly ask him to come back to work. The pigeons fly off with much fluttering of wings.

"Now look wwwwhat yyyou done."

I sit down next to him.

"Gggo away. I aint gggoin back."

My father, a good pub man, always says if you want to persuade somebody to do something buy them a drink. After much thinking, no doubt believing another practical joke is about to pounce, Chester agrees to let me buy him a drink.

"Whhats the catch? Nooobody ever buys me a dddrink."

We go to The Pillars of Hercules, a mock-Tudor pub just off Soho Square on Greek Street. I buy Chester an orange juice and I have a half of Watney's Red Barrel.

"You know what they say about this beer." I say with a laugh in an attempt to relax him. "It's as close to water as having sex in a punt."

He doesn't get it, which is probably just as well.

"They all think I'm fffunny."

I ask him where he lives.

"Peabody Estate, Pimlico. Mee mmmum and me." He giggles. "Do you think I'm fffunny?"

I notice a satirical humorist of the day sitting in the corner with a group of mates. "See that tall fellow over there?" I say. "Now he *is* funny. His name's Peter Cook and he's got the same birthday as me. Funny that isn't it?"

Chester lets out a shriek of laughter.

"Come on let's go back to work." He jumps off the barstool.

We've been back less than half an hour before the bully-boys are at it again. The bastards try to parcel him up.

The evil packer with the pock-marked face wraps him in string and tapes up his mouth. "To send you to Wales where all the queer folk live."

Chester is kicking out in a frenzy. My fellow dispatch lads take no notice, the aloof one staring into space as if in a trance, the others reading newspapers. The chauffeur, who is the Spurs fan, is in his element directing proceedings. The MD's chauffeur clutches his belly as he's laughing so much. But I've had enough. I can't see poor Chester persecuted like this anymore.

"FOR FUCK'S SAKE LEAVE HIM ALONE." I yell and jump on the Spurs fan, pull him to the ground and start kicking him.

The boss races in, his bushy eyebrows twitching more than ever, his face glowing pink. "What the devil's goin' on here?"

It works. Chester is released and sits quietly in a corner. Everyone else is sent out on jobs. Except me!

"I don't want to hear that kind of language no more in here. There are women working next door." He's referring to a middle-aged blousy woman who's something to do with dispatch admin and her pretty assistant of about my age, who looks the spitting image of Jean Seberg in the Jean-Luc Godard movie *Breathless*.

"I'm moving you to cover the fifth floor. You might learn a few manners there." The boss tells me.

You know what, that just couldn't be better. Not only do the directors who occupy that floor get hardly any mail, there's a certain receptionist on the fifth I wouldn't mind getting to know a little better.

FOUR

January 1964

I deliver a minimal amount of mail to the fifth floor six times a day. I think I've got the timing right. The haughty one takes a tea break at 3pm, around the time I need to drop off the afternoon paper in reception. The brunette's name is Antonia, and I just love it when she giggles with all the innuendo of Kenneth Williams. I tell her about the hideous secretaries on the floor, hoping they're not friends of hers. How one threatened to report me for going up a small winding staircase thinking it was a shortcut to the floor above.

"You *are* a naughty boy. Only directors are allowed up there." She purrs. "I'm not sure *what* they get up to, other than fine dine that is."

Apart from enjoy the gourmet delights of the forbidden Directors' Dining Room, I'm not terribly sure what the directors do all day. The floor is carpeted in best navy blue Wilton, and there's an air of secrecy with doors closing quietly, whispered conversations. It feels sacred, like a cathedral.

The directors are an elusive bunch, and I begin to wonder if they even exist. Perhaps the arrogant secretaries are a front for some huge scam. Luckily there's always Antonia to cheer me up. I'd like to invite her out for a drink and I can't help but wonder how old she is. I know she's not married, but she may have a boyfriend. I don't think I can take her to the local agency pub, The Red Lion, or “T Mirrors”, in reference to its Victorian mirrored decor.

I have plans to see a hot new group called The Yardbirds and hear they have a great lead guitarist, Eric Clapton. I consider asking her to come along but can’t really see her rocking away in twin-set and pearls. I imagine Jules Bar, the smart cocktail bar around the corner in Jermyn Street, is more her scene. But that’s not my scene, even if I could afford it. The problem is I can’t really afford much on a pound a day.

I’ve been a trainee in dispatch for four months. I’m beginning to feel like a prisoner of war intent on escape, like one of the characters from the Pan paperbacks I used to read avidly beneath the blankets: *Boldness Be My Friend, Escape or Die, The Wooden Horse, Colditz*. Yet I can’t dig a tunnel or snip barbed-wire fencing in the dead of night. I’ve tried to see Major Millard a few times, but he doesn’t want to see me. I met his assistant, an incredibly dreary man who looks like an undertaker. He said he had a note about me wanting to “evidently” work as a copywriter. For a moment or two I thought I might get a lucky break. He said he’d have a word with Mr. Smaile. The following day I’m given one of the creative floors to deliver mail to. Great! I now don’t even have Antonia, although I can always “pop up there”, as she would undoubtedly say.

The creative department is on two floors, and its inhabitants seem to be able to wear what they want. The cinema and projection facility is where new TV commercials are screened and main presentations take place. The plush cinema is a feature of the agency with a large screen and stainless-steel velveteen armchairs. The Sammy Davis Jr wannabe has this delivery run and isn’t prepared to give it up under any circumstances, particularly as one of the perks is to help with film projects. He visits film production houses in Soho where he can always spot an actor, or better still actress, attending a casting session or recording a voice-over. For a showbiz groupie, this is an opportunity not to be sniffed at – the chance to be spotted himself.

As the creative offices are pretty much open plan with partition half-glass walls onto the corridor, it's easy to see the workers inside. They seem much more interesting than the account execs on the sixth floor, or nobody at all on the fifth. I'm getting the hang of how it all comes together. Copywriting, art, and layout are three separate functions with a definite pecking order. The writers have some writing background, such as a degree in English and are, in their opinion, superior to art, and way above layout men.

The art boys sit behind large easel desks with a giant layout pad in front of them and a mug full of crayons at their side. They look a bit like Dickensian clerks before a costs ledger. Typically a facetious copywriter on his way out to lunch will dump a headline with rough typed body-copy on one of them and say: "Can you knock up a visual idea for this old chum. Shall we say four o'clock?"

Art then comes up with a few ideas, scribbles at this stage, to discuss with an inevitably inebriated writer. The favoured ideas will be shown to the account executive, probably the following day, and the short list will be passed on to layout.

Layout artists are true artisans: beard, sandals, pipe, scrupulously reliable. They turn the scribbles into a magnificent layout or three to present to the client and hopefully sell the idea.

I'm minding my own business, making my last mail delivery to the layout department when I'm pulled up in my tracks, almost dropping my tray in shock as a wobbling blancmange dressed as a ballerina heads toward me: tutu, tights, even a plastic tiara and magic wand with a star on top. But the absurd bit, the touch that rounds it off, are the black elastic-sided Chelsea boots.

One of the art directors, who looks a bit like Mr. Pickwick, has turned into the Sugar Plum Fairy. He staggers and slurs, "Can you please remind me where the board room is? I'm running frightfully late for a very important meeting."

He's been to Monty Berman the theatrical costumier again, his little peccadillo after a good lunch.

FIVE

I've become very friendly with a secretary to a senior copywriter. Joanna is a statuesque girl in her early twenties with an infectious enthusiasm for the underbelly life of Bohemian Soho. There are advantages to still living at home and missing the last train, particularly in winter when it could be classed as attempted murder by hypothermia for a girl not to offer to share her bed in a freezing cold flat. When the party really takes off, and the Metropolitan Line home has closed, I stay at Joanna's place, a scruffy flat she shares with three girls in the back end of Chelsea, an area known as World's End.

Joanna's large, high-ceilinged abode is in a mansion block next door to where Mick and the lads are currently dossing out. They haven't really made it yet. Their cover of *I Wanna Be Your Man* reached No. 12 in the charts, and they've just released *Not Fade Away*. A good 45, in my humble opinion. The Rolling Stones have come a long way from the cramped cellar of the Ealing Jazz Club, and they are the first act to appear on the new *Top of the Pops* television show. Being neighbours, I'd like to tell them how impressed I am, but they seem to keep different hours to me.

I go to the Queen's Elm pub on the Fulham Road quite a bit with Joanna. It's a spit and sawdust boozer with little decor other than a glass case full of clay pipes. Loads of jobbing luvvie actors drink here, together with Laurie Lee, author of *Cider with Rosie*. It's a Guinness pub, and we all drink pints of the glorious black stuff. When last orders are called there's invariably a lock-in, and Bushmills Irish whiskey gets passed around.

It's 2am and Joanna invites a dashingly louche out-of-work actor who has appeared as a galley slave in *Cleopatra* – "I do love working with Burton and Taylor, darling!" – back to her flat and bed. I'm offered the bed of her new flat-mate, a nurse who's on night duty at St Stephen's hospital. I've met her only once: a pretty, well-mannered girl with flaming red hair.

It's so cold. I snuggle in right under the blankets and sleep until I sense someone else in the room. I guess it's about dawn and I'm not feeling great from the mixture of Guinness and Irish whiskey.

A voice at my covered head whispers, "I got out early. Do you want me to keep the uniform on as usual?"

I play dead, wondering what the hell's going on. The voice continues in a comforting, bedside manner. "Now then what seems to be the problem? Do you have the usual symptoms?"

A hand slips under the covers and begins exploring my body. I daren't move. It reaches my vital parts and gets a reaction.

"Is this the little problem? It feels like quite a big problem to me."

Silence for a few seconds as she fondles. "Roger, it is you isn't it?"

She pulls the blanket off my face and lets out a polite little shriek. "Oh, I'm soooh sorry. I thought you were someone else."

Being a well brought up girl she offers to sleep on the sofa. But as it's so cold we come to an agreement – without the uniform.

On Valentine's Night Joanna, who's recently ditched the galley slave, asks me to do Soho with her. "Don't worry, it won't cost. I know enough old soaks to keep us supplied all night."

We start off in a filthy bar that must have once been part of Piccadilly Circus underground station – from the look of the arches covered with stained white tiles, probably the lavatories. The bar's main claim to fame is that Brendan Behan and Dylan Thomas used to drink and fight here. Once again Guinness is the preferred tipple and the Irish barman is proud to say that it's imported straight from Dublin rather than produced up the A40 at Park Royal. "That's why it tastes smoother, it's the Liffey water you know."

Joanna has us talking with a poet and a bookie, who kindly buy the drinks. A few pubs later, and we're at the Colony Room. This small upstairs bar is more a private club and is run by a terrifying woman called Muriel Belcher. Most of the clientele are close to my parent's age and all chain smoke and seem to be completely pissed. Joanna introduces me to the artist Francis Bacon who insists I must be his illegitimate son and tries to kiss me on the lips. He's pouring champagne for all, and then, seeing it's Valentine's Night, he offers to host supper in Wheelers fish restaurant in Old Compton Street. I make sure I sit as far from him as possible as I find him quite terrifying. Eventually Joanna and I catch the last No. 14 bus back to World's End to finish off an opened bottle of Bull's Blood and celebrate St Valentine.

Joanna's boss is an elderly man who likes to dress in tweed and corduroy. He could well pass for a university professor and, thanks to Joanna, he's agreed to see me to discuss my chances of becoming a copywriter, without involving the personnel department.

"Have you ever been published?" He asks.

Before I can answer in the negative he follows this up with, "So tell me, Dear Boy, what are you working on at the moment? A novel or poetry?"

I reluctantly inform him that I am working on neither.

He goes on to tell me that the best copywriters always have a book on the go. "In many ways, that is why they work in advertising, Dear Boy. Knock off a headline and a bit of body copy to pay the rent and then get down to some serious work on the novel, or collected poems if they're so inclined."

Needless to say the discussion comes to nothing.

Deeply depressed, I request another transfer and get the second floor, a place of urgent-looking account execs and an experimental kitchen. The agency is growing and, on the creative side, they have hired a sound-effect specialist, a dapper man with a goatee beard who appears to do little else all day other than... well, mix sound effects – racing cars, storms, surf, steam trains, dogs-a-barking, you name it. He's not too popular with some of the writers as he makes so much noise, which presumably disturbs the creative juices needed for the great tome.

The experimental kitchen is far more straightforward, and the domestic goddess who resides there feeds me. Her job involves creating new recipes to recommend to food clients. The problem is, I can't see any future beyond the food and mail, and sticking up for Chester against the dedicated bullies. There has been a bit of movement. The Jewish guy has gone to work in press production, but it turns out his boss is a rabid anti-Semite who openly calls him a "useless Yid". The aloof one with the hampers has gone into media I think, not that he'd tell me. He did pass on one crumb of information, knowing I'm a bit of a music fan. "Look out for a folk artist called Bob Dylan." He looked as impassive as ever, munching away on a cold drumstick.

It's March and I'm seriously ready to quit. I've been with the agency for six months as a trainee and zilch. Life on the road would be a better option. Or perhaps Mick and the lads could fit me in somewhere since *Not Fade Away* has reached No. 3 in the charts.

Then thankfully, completely out of the blue, a lucky break flutters into my delivery tray.

SIX

I think at this stage I should let you into a little secret, something I don't really talk about. No, it's not one of those "I blame my mother" admissions; this one is entirely the product of my father. He always wanted a son who excelled at sport, preferably playing cricket for England, even captain of the eleven in the mould of Ted Dexter. Sad to say but that son is not I, at least as far as cricket, rugby or football is concerned. I don't actively dislike team sport, I'm just not that good at it. Except for one thing. My father persevered and, being a keen golfer himself, introduced me at a young age to the links at Southport Lancashire – site of one of the nomadic homes we had after our return from Australia. In his mind's eye he no doubt saw me one day lifting the Open claret jug.

So there you are, now you have it: I'm a covert golfer, a secret swinger and, although I say it myself, I'm quite good too. I don't really talk about it to anyone under the age of 25 because it's not exactly cool. Can you imagine me chatting to Mick, "I'm planning to buy a new putter, what about you now you've had some chart success?" Or Joanna and her bohemian gang, "Have you ever written a poem about golf?" I'd be laughed out of town. On the other hand, Antonia may be mildly impressed. When push comes to shove and you're desperate to escape, no holes are barred.

The memo I found myself delivering announced the Spring Meeting of the agency golfing society. I manage to get a blank copy from the nice secretary to the executive who runs the society and I enter my name.

Three weeks later, on a beautiful sunny morning, I arrive at the golf club at 8.30am having travelled by train and then hitched a lift as close to the golf club as I could get. My clubs are in a lightweight bag slung over my shoulder. I've even brought a jacket and tie, assuming, no doubt, they'll be required in the dining room for lunch. Overall I probably look pretty scruffy in my faded Fred Perry polo shirt, an old Pringle sweater and a pair of well-worn corduroy trousers. I enter the lounge where about twenty golfers dressed in immaculate blazers and tweeds are drinking coffee and chatting away in a jovial self-effacing way:

"Haven't played for weeks. I'll be lucky to get off the first tee."

"Had a lesson from that frightfully good chap at Wentworth the other day. He's flattened my swing. More like razed it to the ground I'd say!"

"I see that smooth bastard Piers has turned up again. Complete bandit. We may as well give him the trophy now."

I soon gather that Piers is the bête noir of the society, a super-smooth account director with a substantial private income and low golf handicap. He regularly creams up the trophies, much to the annoyance of the others.

A man in a plus-four tweed suit races over to me and I realise it's the major.

"Good Lord boy, what are you doing here! Come to caddy have you?"

I'm soon teeing off. After a shaky start I find my swing and begin to play like a pro. I win the main trophy, The President's Cup, by an impressive margin. In the afternoon foursomes I'm partnered with Frank, a friendly northern guy who is director in charge of something called the Merchandising Department. I continue my good form and he contributes when needed. We win that trophy too.

At the evening prize-giving there's much mumbling: "Who exactly is he? Which department is he in?"

"A Dispatch lad? Don't be silly, they don't play golf!"

It appears that my card has been well and truly marked. On the one hand, they're delighted that someone has finally beaten Piers. Yet that someone should have been one of them, not a ringer who delivers the mail. Come Monday morning I know I'm going to be fired, as if I'd been caught on the *Directors Only* staircase. But what the hell! It's one way of getting out of the dungeon.

Sure enough an hour after I've started work on Monday, I get the call. The major wants to see me in his office immediately. Needless to say I've not mentioned a word about my secret golf life to anyone in dispatch. I can just imagine the bullies would have a field day on that, taking the pressure off Chester and parcelling me up and sending me off to St Andrews, no doubt. Everyone hears the summons as the boss bellows it from his room.

"Oi! Don't know what you've been up to lad but..."

Although I'm quite prepared for the bullet, I still feel as sick as I did when I first entered the building. If only to take my mind off the forthcoming encounter, I try to work out how I can say goodbye to Antonia. I've kept up our friendship, popping by whenever I think she's alone for a bit of flirtatious gossip. Maybe it'll have to be Jules Bar after all and hang the cost. Perhaps I'll get a week's salary as part and parcel of getting the sack?

The irritating jolly-hockey-stick secretary meets me at the lift and confirms that this is serious business.

"The major is so looking forward to seeing you," she spurts as if she has a mouth full of plumbs. "Gather you had a bit of a humdinger over the weekend. Jolly good show!"

Before I can answer, she's escorted me into the personnel director's office. Straight off, something strange strikes me – the major greets me with a friendly smile. Not only that but he stands up and offers me a chair. What's going on? Perhaps he's read a book on how to fire people with grace and dignity? Or maybe he's on medication?

When we have both settled in our chairs, he gives me a fierce, glazed stare and slams the desk, the routine I saw before I was hired. It seems as if the medication has already worn off.

"Always knew you were cut out to be an account man."

Not for the first time in that office I'm speechless.

"But why on earth didn't you tell me you had this skill when you first joined?"

My mind has gone blank. "Sorry, what skill would that be?"

"Golf, you idiot! Do I have to spell it out for you?"

Before I can say Gary Player, I'm offered a position with immediate effect in the Merchandising Department, as well as a modest salary increase.

"You'll find it a good training ground for being an account man, which will be your next step up the ladder." The major laughs, not something I've seen before.

"Maybe you'll have to win the grand slam of the spring, summer and autumn meetings first though!"

SEVEN

I don't play much recreational golf but turn up for the agency majors, as the major suggested. But now I'm earning a bit more I can afford to visit gigs, which is much more my scene.

Every Friday, I buy *The New Musical Express* to check out the new groups and where they're performing. Luckily, I live in an area full of venues, mostly new ones opening up in the function rooms of large Victorian pubs and hotels. The Richmond Jazz Club at the Station Hotel which, as you might imagine, is opposite Richmond train station; the Ricky Tick in Windsor; The Railway, a pub with a small upstairs room opposite the tube station in West Hampstead.

As well as The Yardbirds there's a London group called The Kinks who are quite good. Georgie Fame and The Blue Flames are the resident group on Saturday nights at The Railway, while a gang of south London nutters called The Who are getting quite a reputation, mainly for smashing things up. The Rolling Stones – or just plain "Stones" as I call them now - recently appeared on ITV's *Thank Your Lucky Stars* and looked pretty silly in matching dogtooth jackets. They've evidently got a manager who used to have something to do with The Beatles – who are still streets ahead in the Mersey sound v. London contest after having four consecutive No. 1 hits.

My new office mate thinks he's a pop star. He also thinks he's Detective Adam Flint from the *Naked City* TV series, particularly when he pushes the green Tyrolean hat he wears to the office onto the back of his head and quotes the signature line:

"*There are eight million stories in the Naked City. This will be one of them.*" He then answers the desk phone, which we share.

I ask him how he came to be known as Willy seeing that his real name is David.

"There I was walking past the stage door of the Victoria Palace Theatre when I come across this bunch of groupies. I told one that I was Frank Sinatra but not to let on. I'm not sure she believed me but all the same she shoved an autograph book in my face. I don't know why but I signed it Wee Willy Harris. I suppose I didn't want to disappoint her!"

For those not in the know, the pop star in question is a short Scottish Teddy Boy who has yet to make it into the charts.

The Merchandising department comprises one large room tucked away on the first floor of the building. I've never actually delivered anything here before. The boss, Frank my golfing partner, has a cubicle of an office in one corner while his secretary sits directly outside. Four merchandising executives each have a desk and their own phone line. Willy and I are the department assistants. Being a few years older than me, Willy is clearly the senior assistant; he also began his career in dispatch.

After my first day, he takes me to the Captain's Cabin just behind Piccadilly Circus. "Let me give you the low-down on the mad house."

He orders a couple of pints of Courage bitter. "The four execs all think they're on the northern club circuit, as stand up comics. As the boss hails from north of Watford he recruits like-minded ex-salesmen. Merchandising is the novelty end of the business, so I guess that makes sense. They created mouse-shaped cat bowls for the pet food account, that kind of thing – but thousands of them. Oh yes, this is big business for the suitcase spivs who supply the goods. Our job is mostly to visit grocery outlets and check the facings, make sure the promotion is being followed through in store."

I buy another pint and ask about the hat.

"My parents were living in Vienna and sent me to boarding school in England with this Tyrolean titfer. I've become quite attached to it. Doesn't it remind you of Harry Lime?"

Willy's final word of advice is to watch out for the practical jokes. The following morning there's a note on my half of the desk to call a certain number and get Mr. Lyon in for an urgent meeting. Of course the number turns out to be London Zoo!

Something called a "Personality Promotion" appears to be the flavour-of-the-month. Colgate toothpaste have a White Knight dressed in white plastic armour trotting around on a white horse handing out samples of their toothpaste. Evidently this has been so successful the merchandising team has plans for an Ajax Power Man. The character is loosely based on Superman: blue and red tunic and cape, the colour of the packaging, with AJAX POWER MAN printed across the chest. There are half-a-dozen of these characters working their way around the country, knocking on doors offering a product demonstration and leaving behind a free sample.

However, a Power Man has been spotted drinking heavily in pubs in the Oxford area and, worse, while giving a product demonstration he made a pass at a very un-amused housewife – not altogether surprising as they are all out-of-work actors. Anyway she reported him to the local fuzz. Word has filtered back to the client who tips us off.

"Do you want him dead or alive?" Willy asks.

No, our brief is to find him and fire him.

So we do a pub-crawl. It makes sense. How else would you track down a ham actor dressed like Superman who enjoys the occasional tipple or six before he begins his rounds knocking up housewives?

Willy, using all his detective nous, suggests we concentrate on pubs with a theatrical connection. Midday has barely struck before we hear a whole load of theatrical bullshit coming from the salon bar of a small pub called The Prince Hal situated in a run-down part of town.

"So I tell Larry he can stuff his Hamlet right up his arse if he expects me to take that kind of crap. Anyway, I always prefer to work with Johnny Gielgud. We're on the same wavelength, you know."

I think he sounds a bit too old for our man. But Willy will hear none of it. "See that long coat he's wearing? I think we'll find a tunic beneath that little number."

The apparent culprit is nursing a large gin and tonic while relaying his thoughts. "Johnny's Old Vic Hamlet will take a great deal of beating..."

Willy doesn't hold any punches. He yells, "Gotcha! I'm from central casting and I here-by dismiss you from our current production of the Ajax Power Man."

The accused looks utterly bewildered. He then starts a tirade worthy of *Look Back in Anger*. That's when the coat falls open to reveal an immaculate tweed suit.

The police eventually rounded-up the real villain running through a housing estate in his Ajax outfit being chased by an angry husband brandishing a shotgun.

EIGHT

February 1965

Now that I'm an executive of sorts I seriously need a new suit. I check out Jaeger in Regent Street, particularly as they've got a photo exhibition of what they call the "rising stars of the sixties". The shots are by a young Cockney photographer, David Bailey, who's going out with the most beautiful girl in the world, a model with the name of Jean Shrimpton. Young actors are included in the exhibition: Terence Stamp and Michael Caine and, blow me down, there's also Mick looking all sexy with pouting lips.

Bailey mostly takes photos for *Vogue*. I flick through *Vogue* and *Queen* magazine when I'm chatting up Antonia - she has most of the fashion mags in reception. Other photographers of the day seem to have only one name: Duffy, Donovan, O'Neill. Cecil Beaton is still going strong; even he has photographed Mick. Antonia likes Beaton. I suppose she would, being a twin-set and pearls kind of girl. In many ways she looks a bit like a model, tall and slim with a fashionably pale complexion. Not that I've seen that much of Antonia's figure as she's generally sitting behind her desk.

I can't possibly afford off-the-peg Jaeger, which is a shame as I really fancy a French blue gabardine number. Carnaby Street, just behind Jaeger, is the trendy new place with a few shops selling some fab gear, but they don't sell suits. I mention the suit issue to my Jewish pal in production. He tells me to get a suit made to measure by a "tailor to the stars", Sam Arkus in Berwick Street, Soho.

"How the hell am I going to afford that?"

After a quick tap dance I'm told, "Just mention my name and you'll get a good price."

They've never heard of my Jewish pal, but I do get a good price for a mid-grey three-piece in soft Donegal tweed. Three fittings are needed. The really stylish execs in the agency all wear three-piece suits, with a slightly draped jacket and slim-line trousers: a Mississippi gambler look, like James Garner in *Maverick*. Now all I need is a pastel coloured shirt from Harvie & Hudson next to the "Hall of Mirrors" pub. Yet as with Jaeger I can't possibly afford their prices. I'll just have to dye a couple of old Rael Brook white ones. Luckily I can just about afford a flowered tie from Liberty.

I'm not a smoker but I have just passed my driving test. Willy can't drive so I get the special assignment on Embassy cigarettes, the top-selling fag in the land. Merchandising has the job of producing an Embassy gift catalogue, which is all kept top secret from the competition.

Basically my job is to deliver and collect the catalogue items from a safe house in Fulham and drive them in a company Ford Cortina estate to a photographer behind Hyde Park Corner. Like Bailey and the rest, he also seems to trade on just one name – in this case it's Reg.

The safe house is owned by the account executive on Embassy, a nice guy who used to be a barrister before turning to advertising. He bought it in a pretty run down area and, as yet, hasn't done it up or moved in. As there are about fifty or so items in the catalogue, mostly things like electric toasters and kettles, it's an ideal storage venue. An unmarked van delivers there once a week, usually after 6pm when it's dark. One night, there was a spot of bother with the neighbours. A couple of hoods knocked on the door, accused our man of running some kind of stolen goods racket and wanted a cut or else they'd inform the cops. Needless to say the barrister in the ad man managed to talk his way out.

Reg the photographer enjoys a drink. By about midday, when his assistant is busy setting up the shot he takes me to the pub just behind his studio in Grosvenor Crescent Mews, the historic Grenadier which the Duke of Wellington used to have a few ales in. It's full of memorabilia of Waterloo and even has a sentry box outside.

The star item to be photographed is a Mini Moke Jeep – a trendy four-seat, small wheel, low-slung mini Jeep. While we're having a drink, Reg's assistant bursts into the pub. Reg goes outside to have a word. After a few minutes he comes back looking worried.

"You're coming to the shoot tonight, aren't you old chum?" He asks.

"Wasn't planning on it." I reply.

"Umm... I think you'll find you are now. Sorry and all that, but we need you."

The photo is a location shot in Leicester Square of a well-dressed couple being chauffeur-driven in the Moke to a red-carpet premiere. The male model has taken ill, and now Reg wants me to step in as the model agency can't find a suitable replacement at such short notice.

"You'll get the fee, and it's good money being a night shoot."

"Okay, you're on Reg. But if anyone I know sees me..."

"Great, old chum. Thanks a million. Nobody will recognize you. And you get to cuddle a half-Russian beauty in the back of the Moke while I snap away up front."

I go to change into the evening kit in Reg's studio, but come out very quickly. "You must be joking! I'm not wearing that!" It's a penguin outfit: white tie and tails.

Reg looks sheepish. "Afraid so, old chum. That's what the shot requires and there 'aint no alternative."

We drive around and around Leicester Square. It's about 8pm and busy. I sit with my arm around Tatiana, her short Vidal Sassoon hair cut ruffled by the wind, her pillar box red lips parted to show the exhilaration of the shot, her long black velvet dress looking out of place against the green metal flooring of the open Mini Moke Jeep.

People stop to look as we pass by.

Reg is in his element, clicking away on his Leica. "That's great. Give her a hug. More sexy, darling. Yes, yes, hold it there… This is your hot date. Yeah, yeah, nice. Hold it there. Got it! Cool. A bit more of the old passion. Just think wotcha goin' to get up to later on. One more time, here we go then. . ."

Thoughts of later on definitely have crossed my mind as leggy Tatiana gets sexier by the minute.

All the shots are in the can, including some of us pulling up outside the Odeon cinema and being helped out by a peak-capped chauffeur. Reg says he wants to take us to a bistro on the King's Road. He knows the owner who will give us a meal even though it's getting late. We grab a taxi and go straight there. Reg's assistant looks after his cameras and film.

Soon, without any warning, it's 2am and we are very drunk, having quaffed cheap brandy with the Polish owner of the bistro. Reg is bundled into the back of a taxi to take him home to his ever-tolerant wife in north London. The owner has called time and I'm alone on the pavement with Tatiana… surprise, surprise having missed my last train home! I'm not so drunk that I've forgotten that she lives on her own just around the corner; or that, although I say it myself, we seem to be getting on pretty well. Reg's words of encouragement keep drifting back... "Just think wotcha goin' to get up to..." The evening is seriously cold. Then I remember what's missing. My overcoat, together with the rest of my kit locked in Reg's studio.

Tatiana's flat is warm and furnished with ethnic rugs and different sized brass candlesticks. She lights each one with a taper to give her sitting room an eastern glow, helped along by the pungent scent of joss sticks. She puts on an LP – *Olé Coltrane*, jazz-saxophonist John Coltrane. I'm impressed.

She pours two glasses of vodka, without even asking if I want one.

"You want to play roulette?" She asks.

"Sure, why not. What are the rules?"

She opens a drawer and pulls out a six-shooter. "Striptease. Russian roulette style."

"I'm on for that."

She breaks the pistol and loads what appears to be one bullet. She spins the chamber, puts the gun to her head and pulls the trigger. BANG! A loud shot echoes around the room. She collapses to the floor.

"JESUS! She's fucking shot herself." I race over to her prostrate body.

She sits up and bursts out laughing. "A starting pistol, dear little mister penguin. Now I'm going to bed, on my own. You can sleep on the sofa if you wish."

I don't even attempt to get undressed, not that I could undo the stiff winged collar. I'm thrown a couple of blankets and her bedroom door slams firmly shut. I can't wait to get out of the flat. The problem is I've got no money. I'll have to walk to Reg's studio, a mile or so at the most.

At eight o'clock in the morning, some school children waiting at a bus stop laugh and point as I pass by, while an elderly woman standing with them asks if I have any Penguin biscuits. A little later a man looking like a tramp asks if I have free samples of sherry to give him. Passing through Sloane Square a policeman asks what I've done with Ginger Rogers.

Working in Merchandising is turning out to be fun!

NINE

Summer 1965

I've been working for almost two years now and I haven't had a holiday. I've taken a week off here and there but mostly stayed at home, visiting a few jazz festivals, which have really become R&B festivals for new bands – The Small Faces, The Kinks – and a few older performers such as Alexis Korner, Long John Baldry, Donovan. The traditional jazz craze of Acker Bilk or the Temperance Seven is now a thing of the past.

Often I go up into London for a night with a friend to visit The Troubadour, a lock-in cellar below a coffee bar. It's on Old Brompton Road, and Bob Dylan played his first London gig here. I went to see another new American folk singer there, Paul Simon, but I don't think he's as good as Dylan.

I go often to the cinema, generally taking a date. The problem is I like to see French avant-garde stuff and I'm not sure the girlfriends really go for that; although I also like James Bond, and the girls fancy Sean Connery. I've seen a new Louis Malle film *Viva Maria*! starring Brigitte Bardot and Jeanne Moreau. I guess that's what's given me the idea to go to France for a proper summer holiday, to visit the new trendy spot where Brigitte and her pals go. The only problem is, as usual, I don't have much money. So I've decided to hitchhike to St. Tropez. On the map, it's not that far, and I'm fairly used to sticking my thumb out to cadge a ride.

Evidently Mick goes to St. Tropez. Maybe he'll pass me on the road and give me a lift. Despite not having me around to load up the transit van, the Stones have really hit the big time with three number ones on the run – *It's All Over Now, Little Red Rooster, The Last Time*. There's a new single about to be released but I guess I'll be on the beach in St. Tropez by then - who knows, maybe even having a beer with Mick and Brigitte?

I catch the midnight ferry across the English Channel to Boulogne. It's a more adventurous way of doing it than a regular day crossing, and cheaper. Most of my fellow passengers look as if they've stepped out of a Graham Greene novel, on some kind of spying mission with a trilby hat pulled down over the forehead.

We disembark in the dark. Even though it's summer, the air in northern France is cold. I walk for what seems like miles with a rucksack and sleeping bag on my back. My guide is one of my parents' old Michelin maps. The time according to my Timex wristwatch is 3am – sorry, make that 4am I've forgotten the time change. I'm the only one hitchhiking and all the traffic from the ferry has passed me by, not even a cheeky hoot of the horn.

At last a small lorry pulls up and the driver offers to drop me a few miles up the road, towards the road to Rouen. Not a great start but nevertheless a lift. I get out of the lorry as dawn is breaking. There's not much traffic about and, after an hour, I must have walked about five miles. I'm getting tired. All I have to eat is an apple or two, and my water flask is running dry. A smart looking Citroen comes along driving at speed. It pulls over to the side of the road just ahead of me. I jog along to catch the car before the driver changes his mind.

I'm offered a lift all the way to Rouen. And the driver speaks good English.

After about twenty minutes he pulls up at a roadside café. "Are you hungry? Would you like some breakfast?"

I'm not sure about this guy. He's in his forties and kind of sleazy. He keeps looking at me in a funny way. But over a much-appreciated free breakfast of ham and scrambled eggs I tell him my plan to get as far as the South of France.

"I have a better plan," he says. "Come with me to Switzerland. That's where I'm heading. You can stay at my chalet for free. We have a good time together, non?"

Shit! How do I get out of this?

"That's really kind of you. But you know what? My mother is seriously ill, dying in fact. I don't know why I'm away. Actually I think I'm going to head back home immediately."

The guy seems pissed off, particularly having just paid for breakfast. He dumps my rucksack on the roadside and speeds off. One of the problems with hitchhiking is you never know who's going to pick you up.

I've been standing thumbing, walking thumbing, standing thumbing for a couple of hours. And it's getting hot. At last, a grumpy lorry driver takes me to the outskirts of Rouen. Enough is enough. It's midday and seriously hot. I'm tired, foot-sore and fed up. I've got money to pay for accommodation. To hell with it, I'm going to spend it on a rail ticket south and sleep on the beach. Otherwise it could take me a week to reach St. Tropez.

I have to change trains a couple of times to reach Antibes. The overnight journey is in a second-class compartment full of men stinking of garlic, smoking Gauloises and playing cards. I get some sleep, but not much. It's really hot in the South of France and everything is a vivid bright colour, the colour you usually see only in the photos of National Geographic Magazine. From the old

Michelin map it seems hardly any distance at all to hitch a lift to St. Tropez. A car with a friendly driver pulls up after a few minutes and takes me as far as Juan-les-Pins.

At this rate I'll be in St. Tropez in next to no time. I treat myself to a nice cold beer, to celebrate the fact that I've made it, that I'm on holiday. I find a small backstreet bar – the ones on the front are too expensive – and sit at an outside table.

After a while a short, thickset man in his mid-twenties approaches me. He looks English, but an Englishman impersonating a French artist: beret, blue and white striped matelot top, paint-splattered jeans and espadrilles.

"Good morning," he says in a ridiculously posh accent. "You look English if you don't mind me saying so. And perhaps somewhat lost? Correct, eh what?"

He offers me another beer, orders one for himself and draws up a chair. "Don't worry old chap I'm not a queer. Quite the opposite in fact. I love women to death. Adore 'em, just can't get enough of the gorgeous creatures and their wondrous ways. That's why I paint 'em, you see. Portraits, that is. Let me introduce myself..."

Tristan has recently quit an Army commission to follow his real vocation in the South of France. Then he comes clean.

"To tell you the truth I'm not that good, but it's a great way to chat up the birds. With a remarkable success rate as it just so happens."

He orders another couple of beers, and I bring out some francs.

"No, put your money away they're on me. Tell you what, why don't you join me as my assistant? A young virile-looking chap like you could increase the strike-rate no end. You've got a sleeping bag so you can kip on the floor in my little studio."

I'm tempted, but feel I must stick to plan A.

"Here's my address just in case you change your mind."

It's now mid-afternoon and the beer has gone to my head. The heat is also getting to me and all I want to do is dive into the clear blue water of the Med, tantalizingly only a few yards away. I get a lift in a vegetable van as far as the next town, Golfe Juan. I've passed great-looking beaches and I haven't even had a swim. Feeling Brigitte can wait I go for a dip.

As I come out of the water a long-haired, bearded guy wearing faded jeans and no shirt approaches me.

"I wouldn't leave your gear here, the cops will confiscate it before you can say, 'jack shit'." He sounds German. "Come to our encampment if you want, you'll be safe there."

We follow a narrow foot tunnel under the railway line that runs along the coast, then up a well-worn trail through olive groves to a dusty field. Three genuine beatniks with girlfriends are lazing in the shade of a mature carob tree. They're German and speak good English. I'm immediately offered a joint. Although I don't smoke I think it would be rude not to join them. Anyway, a joint isn't a cigarette is it? I'm soon feeling giddy and decide to have another swim to clear my head.

Any thought of making it to St. Tropez today is completely out of the window. I stay on the beach until sunset, enjoying the beauty of it all, plus the French girls in their bikinis. I decide to spend the night with the beatniks and head off again early morning, aiming to hit Saint Tropez in time for lunch. When I get back to the campsite, night has fallen and the cicadas have started their singing. The beatniks are also singing to an acoustic guitar, smoking hash and drinking bucket-loads of cheap peasant wine. I'm happy to join in telling them that I'm an art student. I'm not sure 'ad man' is quite their scene.

In the morning I feel like death, with a hangover from hell. I leave the beatniks to their breakfast joints and continue with my plan to hitchhike to St. Tropez. I get a ride straight away from a driver who doesn't understand a word I say, partly the language problem but more my slurred speech. Within a few minutes I'm back where I was yesterday, in Juan-les-Pins. In my hung-over state I was standing on the wrong side of the road, no doubt thinking I was back home. French holiday-makers are flocking down to the beach: sexy bikini-clad girls, smart women in wide-brimmed straw hats and sunglasses as big as saucers, bronzed Adonis-type men looking like Sacha Distel. I'm getting a message: why slog my way down to St. Tropez? It's all here for the taking, in Juan. Anyway, I feel so rough I don't think I'd last hitchhiking in the sun. I decide to look up Tristan, take up his offer to camp out there.

His studio is a dusty basement next to a garage on the outskirts of town. There's one large room with kitchenette, a separate tiny bathroom and a fair-sized bedroom. In return for a roof over my head, wine, bread and cheese I have to be his pimp, to assist him in his sad chat-up routine: "You have floated into my existence like a goddess off the brush of Botticelli. I am but a mere humble artist who is compelled to follow in the master's shadow and attempt to capture such ravishing beauty for time immemorial."

He can't sketch, let alone paint, to save his life. And yes, he is on the pull, big time. Unsuccessfully, I think. And he wants me to act as a bird puller, to pass them on to him when they're so pissed they don't care.

"Got a gorgeous gal lined up who wants a portrait done. Believe she has a pretty friend as well."

The bullshit is relentless, so much so that I now go out for the day by myself, to the public beach.

One evening we're having a beer, which I can't avoid but he's paying, and he gets called into a back room by the proprietor of the bar. His persona seems to change from buffoon back to army officer.

"Won't be a minute. Got a spot of unfortunate business to sort out."

I know there's something decidedly fishy about my new pal Tristan.

I've been with Tristan for three days and I'm not sure I can stand much more. We're having our usual early evening beer when a song comes on the radio.

"This is it." I say.

"What's that, old chum?"

"Shut up. I want to hear this."

"Sounds like some fellow-me-lad in agony if you ask me."

"Tristan, I told you...shut it! I want to hear the record, words and all."

A few seconds silence. Then Tristan starts laughing. "I say! The fellow's singing about not getting enough. Should be my anthem if you ask me!" More laughter. "Is he a black fellow by any chance? Sounds like one to me, all this nonsense about not getting no satisfaction. You know what they say about black chaps..."

That's it! The final insult. I'm off to St. Tropez tomorrow. I've still got a week left. I break the news the following morning.

"That's a shame old chum, thought we were getting on rather well." He persuades me to stay just one more night, using the "I owe him one" card.

"You've got to help me out tonight. A couple of American birds I've been working on. A little older perhaps than I would normally choose but it should be fun. And the really good-looking one is very much looking forward to meeting you."

I return from the beach at about six o'clock, but there's no sign of Tristan. I wait a couple of hours in his studio and still he doesn't pitch up. I go to his favourite bar, where he had his "meeting". A surly waiter who regularly served us says he doesn't know who I'm talking about.

I go back to the studio and decide to leave straight away, to quit while the going's good. I'll take a train to St. Tropez, I've got the money. I reach for the cash I've hidden at the bottom of my rucksack – most of it's gone. Nicked! Without doubt stolen by the bastard, rat, shitbag, arsehole Tristan. If I ever get my hands on him... I hardly have the price of a rail fare to St. Tropez now. And as for getting back to Boulogne? Luckily I still have a return ticket for the cross Channel ferry.

No other choice than to use my suspect skills as a hitchhiker. Brigitte and her clones will just have to wait for another day. And as for Mick? But I do like the new record, as does all of the South of France it would seem. Wherever you go, they're playing *Satisfaction*. Pity it will always remind me of that tosser, Tristan.

TEN

A long, testing hill leads out of Aix-en-Provence. The N7 heading north is busy with French holiday-makers returning home. I had picked up a lift from Juan without too much trouble but I hit a trail of beatnik hitchhikers, all apparently heading in the same direction as me. I'm about number twelve in the queue. I guess it's going to take a week to make it home, just in time to go back to work. Great holiday!

By mid-afternoon, it's blisteringly hot. I walk up the hill to where the road straightens out into a classic tunnel of French plane trees. I've tried to disassociate myself as much as I can from the beatniks by wearing clean and reasonably smart clothes – off-white jeans and a pale blue polo shirt – on the theory that picking up a well-turned out hitcher must be preferable to filthy denim and hair. Yet it doesn't appear to be working as car after car, truck after truck, pass by. Some hoot and wave others slow down to build up my hopes only to accelerate away. I sit down in the shade of a plane tree, tired and pissed-off.

There hasn't been any traffic for a while. I begin to walk again and keep my eyes open for a suitable field to sleep in, which will make two open-air nights in a row.

I hear a car in the distance. From the sound it's heading my way. I turn to look, sticking out my thumb in anticipation. The heat haze makes everything shimmer, I can just about make out a low-slung car. Then, like that scene in *Lawrence of Arabia* when Omar Sharif rides his horse out of a mirage, I see a silver-grey sports car heading my way. No chance! But I start thumbing just for the hell of it.

The open-topped sports car approaches at a steady speed. I can see two people. No room, so forget it. I drop my thumb to gaze at the beautiful couple: a super-smooth looking driver and his drop-dead-gorgeous blonde passenger. Without a doubt she's as good looking as Bardot. For a crazy moment I think perhaps it is her. As the car draws level, cruising at only about 30mph, something silly happens: the blonde in the passenger seat blows me a kiss. I don't know what comes over me but instead of waving, or just standing there embarrassed, I blow one back. After all this is France. The driver stops, pulls over. I've obviously insulted him. Now I'm in for it.

The blonde slowly turns around in her seat to face me. We are about fifty yards apart. She casually takes off her sunglasses, looks directly at me for a few seconds, then effortlessly extends a suntanned arm and beckons me to join her. At first I think of running for it in the opposite direction, not fancying a smack on the jaw from Mr. Cool sitting beside her. He keeps the powerful engine ticking over with the occasional rev. I pick up my rucksack and sleeping bag, take a deep breath, and do as instructed.

Without doubt she is the most beautiful girl I've ever seen. She asks me in French where I'm heading. I reply in English, mispronouncing Boulogne. She then asks me in English, with the pouty delivery of Françoise Hardy, if Paris would be of any help. Am I dreaming this? Have I had too much sun and not enough sleep? At any moment I expect to wake up in a field with a cow licking my face.

She gets out of the car and I see she's quite petite, but looks great in pale blue calf-length hipsters and the short, white leather Courreges flat-soled boots that seem to be all the rage in chic French circles this summer. A white cotton shirt is tied at her waist showing a golden-tanned midriff. She helps me squeeze my rucksack and sleeping bag into the back and then, holding the door open, offers me her seat. In the nicest possible way I ask her where she intends to sit.

She giggles, and then pouts her lips again, in that sexy indignant way that only French girls can pull off. “So, you don’t want to share?”

I apologize and get in before the driver, who hasn’t said a word, changes his mind and tells me to get lost. She slips onto my lap, putting her arm around my shoulder for support.

The car is a Facel Vega and the driver doesn’t hold back as he roars up the N7, keeping his Ray-Bans in place even though it’s now twilight. The blonde is as light as a feather and smells of sun and fresh flowers.

“I like you.” She whispers in my ear as her blonde locks flurry across my face. “You remind me of my kid brother. That’s why I stopped.”

She puts the Motorola car radio on, tuning it to a pop station. “I love your English rock n roll, all the groups you have. Sooo sexy.”

After a while the inevitable happens. “This is my new favourite song.” She says. “Really sexy. And the singer, oh la, la!”

“I sort of know him.”

“Really! You know the Rolling Stones?”

For a second, just a second, my mind flashes to an image of the unsexiest man in the universe: Tristan. And then, like the setting sun it fades away as my new companion wriggles her tight little backside in my groin to the languid rhythm of *Satisfaction*. I can’t help my reaction, and she knows it.

It must be close to midnight. The driver has pulled into a rustic hotel somewhere south of Lyon. Not one for conversation he explains that he’s too tired to continue. The blonde is snuggled into me, asleep. He goes into the hotel and returns a few minutes later. By now my lap-mate has woken up. He talks in French to her. She yawns, shrugs her shoulders and says "Pas de problème." He then addresses me in good English. "The hotel only has one room available."

"That's not a problem. I have my sleeping bag and can camp out in that field over there."

"I wouldn't hear of it." He says. "It's a large family room with a double and single bed. I insist you join us, as my guest."

Here's a guy who has hardly spoken to me and suddenly he's offering me a bed. I'm not sure about this, but I don't fancy a field and… the blonde looks at me and pouts her lips again in her pissed-off way.

I use the communal bathroom down the hallway to allow them the privacy to get into bed. I stay as long as I can. When I creep back into the large family room the lights have been switched off. I take off my jeans and polo shirt and climb into a wrought-iron single bed, next to a window overlooking an inner-courtyard and well away from the outline of an antique double bed.

Silence. Darkness. As soon as my head hits the pillow I'm asleep.

I wake to the sound of a courtyard clock striking seven times, rays of sunlight touching my face through flimsy curtains. Suddenly I'm instinctively aware of someone watching me. I discreetly turn my head towards the far side of the room and the double bed. On the floor, a scattered trail of clothes and underwear lead to the bed. Her clothes: the boots, hipsters, shirt, bra and pants. No sign of any men's clothes. Perhaps they are on the other side, or have been neatly folded away?

She's alone in the double bed, sitting up with a white sheet held up to her neck by a suntanned hand. She's wide awake and staring at me, head slightly to one side. Without saying a word she beckons me to join her. A thousand thoughts race through my head all at the same time; not the least of which is where the hell is the driver? And what if…?

I don't know why but I can't stop that song falling onto the turntable in my mind. *Satisfaction* kills off any hesitation. I do as I'm directed. She whispers in my ear not to worry, that it is perfectly all right, because I remind her of her brother. She takes me in hand and guides me into her, giggling as if it is all just a naughty romp.

Feeling a touch guilty, to say the least, I eventually find the driver downstairs in the restaurant having breakfast and sorting out the bill. I have no idea what the relationship is; perish the thought they are married, although she isn't wearing a wedding ring. Over a coffee and cognac he eases my conscience: no serious involvement, a model friend he's taken to St. Tropez for the long weekend.

"Have you ever been there?" He asks.

ELEVEN

February 1966

I've been promoted to an assistant account executive on the Mobil Oil account. I'm nineteen and a half years old and have finally made "suit". It wasn't entirely down to my remarkable ability at the ad game, I also had to perform on the golf course again and win the Captain's Bowl and the President's Cup for the second time. I'm young for the role and fortunate that my account executive boss used to be a prep school master, so he has endless patience in teaching me the job. Not that you can teach the art of persuasion in the same way you can teach, say, algebra.

Persuasion comes in many forms, as I'm fast learning. The finished product has to be a piece of persuasion to get someone to buy, or buy into, something they don't necessarily need. Before that, the client has to be persuaded that what the agency has come up with is an answer to all his needs. Prior to that comes my main job: to persuade a bunch of difficult, lazy bastards to actually do some work and produce ideas for advertising, and a plan on where, how and at what cost to place the ads, if they ever get approved and produced.

As easy as pie really!

My main problem though is my age: I look young for my years. Yes, it's great to have made it from the dungeon and onto the account executive ladder in little over two years, but the pressure is on. I'm on the front line now rather than larking around behind the scenes. I've bought a few more made-to-measure three-piece suits by Sam Arkus. They are in dark materials to make me look older, and I've taken to smoking Wills Whiffs small cigars when I meet with a difficult copywriter, one whose opening line could well be, "Piss off, Junior. Get back in the cradle. Can't you see I'm busy!"

As I'm not really a smoker I cough and splutter, which is no good when you're trying to be firm and insist the copy is written within twenty-four hours.

So I give up on the Whiffs. I also have to write contact reports of meetings, both internal and those with the client. Again my boss has been a great help with jargon and teaching me how to précis conversations.

The agency has installed a brand new system of dictating machines, very progressive. Each account exec's office has a brown Bakelite telephone for dictation. This is transmitted to a pool of typists and, within a few hours, the finished document is magically delivered to your office. If anything is not quite clear, the terrifying woman who runs the pool will pay a visit to sort things out. She has every intention of getting it right first time as she comes from the Hattie Jacques school of diplomacy, the formidable hospital matron from the *Carry On* films. Rumour has it that the typing pool is full of good-looking birds who aren't allowed out, guarded like demure princesses by a dragon in a very large dress.

A new account executive has joined and is in the office next to ours. Apart from the fact that he's evidently a good golfer he's also a complete twit, endlessly boasting about his female conquests and doing very little work. Worse still, he fancies Antonia and keeps telling me that he's definitely going to score there. Of course he missed the training session on the dictating system, evidently having a golf lesson at the time at Simpsons of Piccadilly, the quality-clothing store for men with a golf academy in the basement.

He goes straight from there to lunch at Quaglino's with one of his new girlfriends, an American cabaret singer.

"Thought I'd pop back into the office, make a few calls, even though I was invited to spend the rest of the afternoon in the Hilton." He tells me. "What's this new fangled telephone thing I've got?"

I explain how it works, exaggerating the delights of the beauties at the other end of the line.

Twit-face also fancies himself as a singer in the style of Matt Monro or Frank Ifield, a seriously square crooner who also yodels. He's clearly had quite a few Gordon's G and T's and no doubt some Riesling over lunch.

"My Frank Ifield really gets the birds going, particularly the old yodelling bit. I imagine it's a bit like a mating call." He boasts.

Without much persuasion I get him to sing a song to the typists.

"Just pick up the receiver, press play and off you go. Why don't you dedicate the song to the sexiest one?" I give him the name of the dragon supervisor.

He picks up the receiver and begins with an over-the-top dedication: "To the most scrumptious, hot-blooded gal in the agency..." Then he begins to sing Frank's 1962 No. 1 hit, *I Remember You*, but changing some of the words.

He doesn't make it to the chorus. Hattie, the dragon, bursts into his office like a charging bull, clocks him one in the face and drags him off to an audience with Major Millard. Next thing I hear he's resigned. I'm not a spiteful person but he really did deserve it.

The agency is doing really well, picking up endless new business by trading on its pukka British credentials. More and more account men are needed to handle the growing list of clients. Some of the new account guys are only in it for a bit of a laugh: chinless wonders, failed actors, even a mad monk or two. It's not unusual to find an impromptu game of rugby taking place down a corridor, or cricket with a rolled paper ball. I steer clear of the nonsense. I guess I had enough of that in dispatch. There again, I think I've caught something bigger than a rugby ball, I think I might have captured ambition.

While missing the last train home can have its benefits I desperately want to have my own pad in town. It's still winter and probably not the best time to rent a room, particularly in a flat without any heating. I decide to share a basement flat in Hollywood Road, just off Fulham Road, with a stranger who I hardly ever meet – I think he's a trainee solicitor of about my age but whenever I say hello he shoots into his room like a startled rabbit.

The accommodation couldn't be further from the star-studded image of Hollywood. Keeping clean is a bit of a problem as the bathroom is like a broom cupboard, so small there's only room for a hip-bath. Hot water comes through an antiquated Ascot gas heater feeding off a money-in-the slot meter in the entrance hall. No change, no hot water. Not enough change and the hot water runs out.

The real feature though is the outside lavatory.

I've taken a few girls back to my pad after a bistro meal at somewhere such as Luba's in Knightsbridge, where you can take your own wine. I try to cover for the outside facility by asking them before we leave Luba's, "Do you need the loo before I get the bill?" This has to be delicately, yet purposefully handled. Despite the basic surroundings, helped by a bit of romantic candlelight and Bill Evans on the piano, things generally go well back in my pad: clothes abandoned, the small single bed occupied. But there's always that nagging worry, particularly in the winter.

My worst fears come to pass when a posh girl I really like whose dad owns half a county needs to use the lavatory in the middle of the night. I've dated her a few times and ended up back at her place but on this occasion she wants to see my "Hollywood" pad. She puts on my dressing gown and goes to the bathroom. It's perishing cold, and she's soon back, asking the inevitable question. "You must be joking!" She pulls on her boots, skirt and polo neck for a Captain Oats style departure to the outside loo. And yes, it is snowing! Like Captain Oates, she doesn't return to bed. She gathers up the rest of her things, puts on her maxi coat and braves the blizzard to hail a taxi back to a nice warm flat in Chelsea. That was the last I ever saw of her. And after a couple of months I've had enough. Either the loo moves in, or I move out.

The schoolmaster boss is pleased with my progress and, after a suitable probation period, recommends promotion to an acting account executive of Mobil marine and agricultural oils – something he wants shot of so he can concentrate on the automobile side, in particular petrol. He's recently run a major consumer promotion working with my old colleagues in Merchandising. Being very much old school, he was in his element sourcing a vintage Bentley as the star prize in a competition linked to Mobil petrol. It was a great success and they plan to repeat it with a Rolls Royce, so he'll be off again soon, touring the country like Lord Montagu of Beaulieu checking out vintage Rollers.

My immediate client is a delightful guy in his early twenties. He's another double-barrelled number but not in the least pompous, more charmingly vague and self-effacing. The relatively small budget is spent in specialist magazines, trade press and on technical leaflets. Thankfully the creative people working on the business are professional old lags, never getting in the least bit stroppy about having to write and design a dull detailed leaflet on the benefits of a new tractor lubricant.

We have a pretty good system worked out. We meet in the late afternoon, then rattle through business so we can take a short walk to the club in Pall Mall, where the client is a member, for a swim and drinks. The swimming pool at the RAC Club is all mosaic tiles and Roman columns, with a compulsory canvas thong to swim in. Unfortunately, no women are allowed! And when I say drinks afterwards, I mean a bucket load of beer and gin. His boss is happy with the work, and my boss is happy that his boss is happy. They are even talking of increasing the budget, so the agency boss is also happy at the thought of more income.

Christmas is only a few weeks away and the client wants to buy me dinner at the club as thanks for all the good work.

"How many do you want to host? All the creative guys?"

He turns a mild shade of pink. "Actually if you don't mind I think just the three of us would make a jolly group."

"I think my boss would love to come along. He's always on for a good meal and a few drinks."

A deeper shade of pink. "Errr, it wasn't actually him I had in mind. On Thursday evenings ladies are allowed in the dining room and I thought it would be nice to invite that charming young lady in reception. She's always most helpful."

Now I get it. So that's why he always likes to meet in the agency rather than his Victoria office. My shy, retiring client has a thing for Antonia, the serene brunette I've secretly fancied like crazy yet haven't even summoned up the courage to invite for a drink. And he wants me to pimp a date for him. Is this all part of a full service agency, I ask myself? Lying through my teeth, I say she isn't my type but I'd see what I could do, having first reassured him that she was single, lives in London and I don't think has a steady boyfriend.

Antonia arrives at the RAC at eight o'clock, spot on time. The client and I have passed the previous hour in the bar; in his case, taking on board gallons of much needed Dutch courage. Antonia's been home to change. I've always assumed her home to be Knightsbridge by the way she often refers to shopping in Harrods. She now looks a completely different person to the twin-set and pearls debutant. In fact, she looks as if she's just stepped out of Barbara Hulanicki's trendy new Biba store on Kensington High Street. A military-style maxi coat is handed to the front porter to reveal a silk top, short skirt and brown suede thigh-length boots. Her hair hangs straight in the style of Julie Christie.

My client gulps and whispers in my ear, "Oh my Lord! I'm not sure I can go through with this."

As if to compensate for his nerves our host fills himself and us up with copious quantities of good wine. Antonia is great company, her husky tones giving way to an even huskier giggle. We gossip about the agency and some of the characters. Yet despite drinking like a fish she's discreet, occasionally purring like a mysterious cat hinting at what may just lie behind the serene veneer. I have no clue what my client is thinking. Maybe he's planning the great seduction, which really pisses me off. If he lays a hand on her... But he's all babbling banter and impromptu horse laughs that echo around the formal dining room like a drunk in a giant cave.

Eventually he gets the bill. It's about eleven o'clock.

"Anyone fancy a spot of dancing?" He asks.

I feel sure Antonia will opt out and take a taxi the short distance back to Knightsbridge. That'll mean I'll be left with the client who seems to want to dance, which in his world is likely to be more Victor Sylvester than Chubby Checker. But rule number one for the good account man: never leave until the client has had enough.

"What a super idea!" Antonia says.

We are within walking distance of a number of new and trendy clubs: Scotch of St James's; the Bag O'Nails; Sibylla's, a few yards from Piccadilly Circus; or the more up-market and exclusive Annabel's in Berkeley Square. With the exception of Annabel's, which attracts the young, titled, black-tie, backgammon gang, the others are regularly stuffed full of beautiful people dressed in the latest Carnaby Street gear. On any night you might bump into one of the Beatles, or Mick with Marianne Faithfull, or Jean Shrimpton and her new boyfriend actor Terence Stamp, or Twiggy with boyfriend Justin de Villeneuve. Or even Rudolf Nureyev dancing in the shadows to the Stones. To me, those dim-lit, smart cellar clubs with crushed-velvet banquettes and postage-stamp dance floors must be the check-in point for the real Swinging London. Interestingly, my un-cool client has just joined one of these clubs.

Some time after midnight, the client discreetly pays the drinks bill, kisses Antonia on the cheek and bids us farewell saying he's had the best night he can remember. I find myself alone with Antonia. We are standing outside Scotch of St James's, just behind Jermyn Street, and it is trying to snow. Somewhere in the distance a drunk is singing *Oh Come All Ye Faithful*. In my mind I'm still holding Antonia close to me as we dance to *Here, There and Everywhere* from the Beatles *Revolver*. I certainly wasn't cold then. Now I'm frozen to the marrow, as I appear to have misplaced my overcoat, probably left at the RAC.

"Presumably you've missed your last train home?" Antonia asks in a matter-of-fact way. "I can put you up if you like. I live just walking distance away. Anyway I'm concerned hypothermia may get to you soon."

We cross Piccadilly Circus into Shaftesbury Avenue. The only signs of life are the giant neon advertising signs flashing their eternal messages to *Drink Coca Cola* or smoke *Player's Please*. A few paper party streamers litter the ground around the statue of Eros, one draped over the archer's bow.

After a couple of hundred yards we stop next to Cecil Gee, the men's outfitter. Antonia takes keys out of her handbag and opens up a small door directly next to the shop. She has trouble finding the light switch. When the naked light bulb eventually illuminates the passageway I notice it is run-down and smells of musty and stale cooking. Okay I'm pretty drunk, and my receptionist friend must be equally well away. But what the hell is going on? Where are the twinkling lights of Harrods, the carpeted foyer of a mansion block?

Another door is unlocked at the end of the passageway.

"Here we are." She whispers in her husky voice. "I'm afraid it's a little small but it's terribly convenient for work."

We enter a bed-sit, with a tiny kitchenette and separate bathroom. One large bed is pushed against a wall, with cushions scattered over it to double as a sofa. The only other furniture is a wardrobe, a table and a couple of dining chairs.

She lights two large candles in elaborate candlesticks on the table, the kind you would normally see on an altar, and puts on an operatic LP.

"I do so love *The Marriage of Figaro*, it's such a naughty story." She says in her customary sexy purr.

I've no idea what she's talking about.

She pops into the bathroom.

"Won't be a minute."

I sit on the edge of her bed-cum-sofa. True to her word she shortly reappears. The problem is she's still wearing the maxi coat done up to the neck and boots. She looks at me quizzically.

" So, shall we get going then?"

"Where are we off to?" I ask. Maybe now we're heading for Knightsbridge, and she just wanted to collect her keys from here.

"Don't be a silly billy."

She begins to unbutton her coat. It drops to the floor. She's stark naked except for the thigh boots, her pale beauty caught in the light of flickering alter candles. Jesus! The opera music is still playing. Is this really happening, or am I in a Fellini movie scene?

"Cherubino's aria, my favourite and so wicked." She says as I'm pushed back onto the bed. Again I have no idea what she's on about.

As far as I know the *Beano* is a comic, not a bloody opera song. Before I know it the serene receptionist is straddling me, buttons being ripped open, months of innuendo and flirting coming to its head.

I know she likes reading *Horse and Hound*, but that was crazy. And as for the Cadbury's Flake stuff. In the morning I promise never to say a word, to keep our secret a real secret. I think I'm finally beginning to understand that we are living at a time when what you see is not always what it appears to be, the very essence of advertising, you could say.

TWELVE

August 1967

An estimated 100,000 young people have converged on the Haight-Ashbury area of San Francisco for what their leaders call, “a phenomenon of cultural and political rebellion”. The way they achieve this is evidently through music, psychedelic drugs and free love.

The age of the hippy has arrived with a new laid-back generation who preach “flower power”.

The Monterey Pop Festival got things going in the USA, with bands such as Jefferson Airplane, The Jimi Hendrix Experience, Otis Redding, The Byrds, The Grateful Dead, Janis Joplin and our own south west London nutters who I used to see doing pub gigs: The Who. The launch pad for the whole gig you could say was our own “Fab Four” who released the most extraordinary, fantastic LP I have ever heard, *Sgt. Pepper's Lonely Hearts Club Band.* Now everything is psychedelic images – in art, fashion and pop. The trail along the King's Road, Chelsea, is a kaleidoscope of coloured silks and flowers, men in red military tunics, and micro-mini skirts worn by birds all looking like George Harrison's wife, Patti Boyd.

I'm spending far too much time on a trading estate in Brentford, Middlesex. The silly thing is the better you become at your job, the worse accounts you are assigned.

These blue-chip pieces of business are regarded as an honour to work on but have dull clients in even duller buildings discussing the dullest imaginable sales facts and figures. No sense of humour, just tiresome grind. I'm now an account executive on a large food and drinks account. The senior client is a shit of the first order: he will call a meeting and fail to turn up; keep you waiting for hours while he deals with some "important business"; ask for overnight copy changes at 5.30pm knowing the writers have gone home. The guy is a natural born bully who learnt his skills in colonial Africa and for some reason loathes advertising. Rumour has it he was fired from an ad agency in his younger days.

The client's office overlooks the Great West Road, the route out to Heathrow Airport, and while he dishes out his venom, I daydream of travelling – grabbing a taxi to the airport and catching a flight anywhere, provided it's as far away from Brentford, Middlesex, as possible.

India, that's where I want to visit; everyone is banging on about India, including the Beatles who are following some bearded guru called the Maharishi Mahesh Yogi. George even played sitar on *Revolver* and *Sgt. Pepper.*

Three account pals in the agency are about to set off on their travels. They are all a few years older than me, but I'm jealous nonetheless. I have pints with them in "The Hall of Mirrors", where they plan their travels using an old school atlas, like Victorian explorers in a quintessential Victorian pub. One is heading for South Africa, another to the Far East and the third to Australia. Meanwhile I'm living back home as I can't afford to rent a decent flat and don't fancy another winter of outside loos and icicles hanging from the ceiling.

In addition, I have to sit through the greatest business torture of all, a Nielsen presentation. This monthly sales audit is commissioned by the client and presented to him by pedantic lecturers in bow ties, who spin it all out for what seems like days. The agency has to hope that sales are actually increasing as a result of an advertising campaign. This, of course, is not the main purpose of the audit. The client's extensive list of products is analyzed in every conceivable way: price, region, town, outlet, sex, time of the month...you name it. Graphs and charts come at you from every direction. And I'm the poor sucker who has to sit through it all. The shit of a client, the marketing director with his squinty, foxy face and enough chips on his shoulder to feed the British Army, is in his element. His audience are his gofers, his product managers. And me.

"Fat load of good your advertising has done! If I'm reading the graph correctly it seems that sales in Newcastle have actually gone down following your so-called clever ad campaign there. How about if the agency pay for it? Perhaps you'd like to suggest that to your posh boss. And where is he by the way? Off shooting grouse again?"

My boss is a tall, languid Old Etonian ex-guards officer. Without doubt a case of chalk and cheese when compared to our client. The products are a bottled fruit drink, a slimming drink and an as yet undefined drink of pure lemon juice. On the bottled fruit drink, the brief was to emphasize the naturalness of the product, oozing in vitamin C.

Our creative team, a tough Aussie female writer and her young spaced-out art director who spends his days reading *Winnie the Pooh*, went to visit the factory in beautiful Forest of Dean. They were so taken by what they saw as elf-like men beavering away in a forest they created the idea of a mystical land with photos of the forest shot slightly out of focus, while the body copy explained the unique qualities of the product.

Presenting creative work to a client is often a tricky business, particularly those clients whose creativity stretches as far as painting by numbers.

After a pregnant silence the charming client says, "Nice joke. Can I see the real shots now?"

"No joke. These are the real shots." My boss replies.

"I never thought you lads from a privileged background had much humour, but that really *is* funny!"

"They are not supposed to be funny. They present the majesty and mystery of the place where your fine product is made."

"Don't lecture me, sonny Jim. I could have taken better shots myself with a Box Brownie."

"Sorry but, with respect, I think you are missing the point."

"Missing the point! There's very little point to miss. The photos are out of focus. End of story."

"But surely they remind you of something wonderful, something ethereal and creative."

"There's no need to get clever with me. Go on then, seeing as you're so smart what do they remind you of?"

A thoughtful pause from my boss. "They remind me of Beethoven's Pastoral Symphony...I think the fifth movement, the calm after the storm."

We are thrown out of the office with a demand for a reshoot, at the agency's expense.

Luckily the pictures didn't have to be reshot as the heavy guns sorted it out. The agency chairman and the client chairman had lunch together. But that left us with a wounded client who hated the agency more than ever.

November. Almost a year has passed since our tryst. True to my word I haven't breathed a word to anyone. We continue our mildly flirtatious relationship whenever I pass through reception, and I see her still as a serene brunette in twin-set and pearls. And when I've passed through the double glass doors out into the hallway and nobody is looking, I pinch myself. I've invited her to my twenty-first birthday party but she's spending that particular weekend in Gloucestershire.

Reg has let me have his studio for the birthday bash, provided he's invited and he can ask a whole load of models.

"Course not Reg, couldn't think of anything worse!"

A Friday night in mid-November and the invitation is probably quite disgusting, designed, written and printed by an art director mate at the agency.

YOU ARE INVITED TO A MIGHTY COME-IN. Bring bottles, birds, blankets, family planning aids! (You may be home for New Year, but no guarantee).

And they have all turned up. As well as my own pals, the studio is crammed full of model hippies in kaftans, beads, Afghan waistcoats, flowered Liberty pattern dresses, cheesecloth and denim everywhere. Although the hippies in California held a funeral for the "summer of love" last month, you could believe it was only just beginning in Grosvenor Crescent Mews, Belgravia.

Psychedelic images slither over the walls. The music of the night is all great chart-busting anthems of the year blasted through giant Marshall speakers courtesy of a drugged-out DJ: *All You Need is Love* and *Let's Spend the Night Together* mark the early rivalry of two groups destined for universal fame.

I've invited an angelic young hippy with flowers in her hair to spend the night with me in Reg's darkroom. The music is wonderfully deafening with *A Whiter Shade of Pale* sounding like some heavenly call to paradise. I lead her down a narrow corridor behind the main studio area. A closed, reinforced door leads into the darkroom. I push it open.

"Here we are. Reg won't mind."

Procol Harum have hit their organ solo.

Above the glorious melody I can just make out the voice of my angelic hippy, "You know what? You should try being a hippy before you get too old."

Hang on, I'm only 21!

Then the door shuts and I hear the click of what distinctly sounds like a deadlock mechanism. Suddenly it's pitch black, and deathly silent.

"Are you there?" I call.

No reply. I feel my way along the wall until I find a switch. An ultra-violet light throws the room into a spooky hue. The terrible truth dawns: I'm alone. Not only that, but the door is well and truly locked.

I start to hammer on it. "Can anyone out there hear me?"

This just can't possibly be happening! I'm locked in at my own party with nobody to keep me company.

I'm eventually found and released by Reg quite a few hours later, but all the action is pretty well over. And there's no sign of the hippy with flowers in her hair.

Christmas is closing in fast, as are the party invitations. The art buyer is a pal who is invited to photographic studios, model agencies, art studios. He came to my birthday bash so is only too happy to return the favour, as many times as I can manage to stagger along to drink free booze and chat up a model or two. The other source of invitations is the print production department. I'm quite friendly with the print buyer, through the Embassy catalogue work and golf. The print parties, hosted by printers who have made a small fortune out of the agency, tend to be more formal affairs, with fine quality food and wine, held in the banqueting suite of a good hotel.

I've decided to give a print party a go and I'm allowed to take a guest. Sarah is a copywriter who I'd like to know a little better. She's quite sophisticated and lives in Hampstead. It's Friday night and the weekend beckons, hopefully to be spent in Hampstead with walks on the heath and drinks in the Flask pub alternating with the comfort of Sarah's flat.

We go to the "Hall of Mirrors" for a couple of drinks before setting off to the party venue in Bayswater.

As soon as I've got the drinks Sarah shrieks, "Oh look, there's Peter! We must go and say hello."

We move through to the back bar where Sarah greets and kisses a good-looking man in a brown tweed overcoat and flat cap. He's drinking a pint of Guinness and is reading through what looks like a script.

"Peter, meet Peter." Sarah says.

I recognize him straight away. Of course, it would be extremely bad form to treat Peter O'Toole in any other way than a normal bloke I've just bumped into in a bar.

Sarah knows him from the Hampstead social scene, and he's been rehearsing a new play around the corner.

"We're off to a party, why don't you join us?" Sarah says, even though my invitation is strictly for one guest, not two. So here I am about to take a legendary hell-raising, drinking buddy of Richard Burton and Richard Harris to a party he's not actually invited to.

As if we were being admitted to an exclusive party at the Ritz, a surly bouncer dutifully checks Sarah and my names off his list. Not being the brightest star in the universe he doesn't seem to have noticed that we are actually three.

Sarah appears to have taken the evening over. She links arms with her actor friend and me, thanks the bouncer and attempts to enter.

"Ere, just a moment. I've only got two names down. No more allowed in. The geezer in the cap will have to clear off."

Sarah is not amused. “How dare you! Have you any idea who this... *geezer* as you call him... is?”

The bouncer looks blankly at her.

“Peter darling, do tell this officious little oaf exactly who you are!”

I’m getting a sinking feeling in my stomach, certain that things are about to turn nasty at any moment. Peter O’Toole removes his flat cap and performs a theatrical bow worthy of The Old Vic.

“It is a great pleasure to meet you, sir.” He begins, his pale blue eyes twinkling full of Irish charm. “Let me introduce myself...I’m...I’m Lawrence of Arabia.”

The bouncer’s eyes narrow. “I don’t care if you’re the sodding King of Siam, you ‘aint coming in here mate. Orders is orders, and I don’t see no Lawrence of Arabia on my guest list.”

Quick as a flash, O’Toole ducks beneath the bouncer’s outstretched arm, and legs it into the heart of the party. Sarah and I follow leaving the bouncer shouting abuse. The actor sheds his coat, grabs a terrified-looking girl and sweeps her onto the dance floor. He’s now doing a poor imitation of a tango to *Flowers in the Rain* by the Move. The girl faints, possibly because unlike the bouncer she’s recognized Lawrence of Arabia. The bouncer has now caught up and pounces, with a support team. They chuck O’Toole out into the cold night air, his coat and flat cap thrown after him. He hails a taxi without bothering to say goodbye.

I do feel a bit guilty but Sarah tells me not to, “He’s used to that sort of thing.”

We don’t stay long ourselves, heading off to Hampstead as a better bet.

THIRTEEN

February 1969

A bitterly cold day, and I'm in my client's office being briefed on how he is going to reposition his lemon juice as a female beauty aid.

There are four of us from the agency, including our creative team. Yet again I watch the traffic heading towards Heathrow airport, wondering about those who are flying away to some far and distant land. I have a sister who's nine years older than me. She returned to Australia as soon as she was old enough. That was twelve years ago. I've heard on the grapevine that my Victorian explorer pals are all having a ball overseas – Cape Town, Hong Kong, Sydney. And I'm stuck here in Brentford, Middlesex on a bitterly cold day discussing lemon juice.

I feel 1968 passed me by without too much happening. The Beatles went to India to study Transcendental Meditation with their Yogi pal and came back with another incredible LP: a double one that everyone calls the *White Album*, for obvious reasons. Meanwhile the Stones are getting wilder and wilder, living a life of drugs, sex and rock 'n' roll to the full. In the spring, I moved temporarily into a flat run by Willy of the Tyrolean hat, who has left advertising to seek his fame and fortune in the meat trade, ("I've always had an eye for a raw carcass. Reminds me of when I was in Vienna and this body was pulled out of the river...") The trouble is, as well as being a delightful fantasist, he collects strays, people he meets in the pub and invites to stay.

The flat is large, the top half of a five-storey Edwardian building on the Cromwell Road, Earl's Court. I have my own room, an oak panelled affair that I call the "Tudor room".

One of my favourite lines is to say that it's haunted. You'd be surprised by how many girls want to see a real live ghost. Yet there is a limit to how many bodies you want to step over in the morning, all kipping on the floor of the living room, or sprawled out on sofas. An American guy came for two nights and two months later he's still with us. He's installed his stereo system and, being a classical music fan, blasts Beethoven, Brahms or Liszt every morning.

"Brahms and Liszt" is how most of us are by the end of the evening, on cheap Spanish wine and pipkins of beer. We also have a plague of mice, which girlfriends don't find amusing. Another flat mate has invented a humanist mousetrap involving a plastic bucket. Each morning he gathers up the captured mice and puts them in his briefcase to release in the City, where he works.

The rent isn't much and I plan away fixtures as often as I can, if only to avoid the hysterics when a girlfriend finds a bucket full of wriggling mice in the kitchen each morning.

Advertising research has indicated that women feel most vulnerable first thing in the morning. Based on these findings, the agency has come up with a print campaign for the lemon juice drink. Ads will appear as a full-page advertisement in woman's magazines. The visual shows an elegant woman in her early thirties in a white dressing gown, long natural blonde hair cascading down her back, looking at herself in a hand mirror. French windows lead from her bedroom onto a lush, green English garden. An early morning summer haze suggests the start of a beautiful day.

The headline reads: *7am. The True Test.*

Short body copy points out the potential female dilemma of that "first peek in the mirror", and suggests that a small glass of our lemon juice taken first thing can release a woman's inner beauty and reveal the natural loveliness each woman has to show in the day ahead.

The client loves the concept. But there comes the twist, you could even call it a twist of lemon.

"Fantastic idea! In fact it's so good I want it to appear in the magazines as soon as possible, certainly by May to pick up on the whole idea of an English beauty and a perfect English summer morning."

A devilish grin, followed by, "That shouldn't provide a problem should it? I mean surely experts like you can sort anything out."

You only have to look out of the window and see the large flecks of snow beginning to fall from a slate-grey sky to get the point.

Magazines have long copy dates, particularly for full colour, often as long as three months. It doesn't take a genius to work out that we've set ourselves a near-impossible task, one the shitty client will wallow in as the agency tries to figure out how to photograph a perfect English summer garden at dawn, in mid-winter.

A studio shot isn't on because of the harsh light and superficial look. The South of France doesn't have the weather; South Africa, Australia, California haven't got the right setting or light, plus we don't have the budget to travel there. Thankfully, out of the blue, our art director, an experienced old lag who knows most things in the creative world, comes up with a good solution. A fairly quirky one, but at least it's a solution.

"There's this island you see, off the coast of Ireland that is, that has summer all the year round."

To begin with we think he's been on the Guinness.

"No, have a look at this."

Photos of a typical English lush country garden taken in the grounds of a house on a small island off the fishing village of Glengarriff on Bantry Bay, south west Ireland.

"And those pics, believe it or not, were taken in March, when there was snow on the mainland. It's a phenomenon all down to the Gulf Stream. The island has a temperate climate, with green Irish grass and lush summer shrubs. Oh yeah, they can't avoid the rain though, Gulf Stream or not."

Now here comes the punch, but a nice punch, more biff than knockout blow. The client insists that a new product manager attend the shoot. He's a steady guy, a safe pair of hands who could make Val Doonican look like Little Richard. A rule of clients attending a photo shoot is that an account man also has to attend to act as minder. And that account man, on this occasion, just so happens to be me. The photographer is an old buddy of the art director, a Scot who enjoys a drink or three. The model is Australian, chosen for her natural beauty.

An inquisitive head pops up out of crystal clear water, a diver with long sagging whiskers. I put my hand in the water. It's unbelievably cold. Even with a wet suit on, he must be frozen. But it's not a diver at all. None of us are functioning too well, which is only partly due to the fact that it's only 5am.

The seal swims towards our boat to have a closer look at our five shivering figures and the one hearty boatman seemingly impervious to the Irish chill. It then dives beneath a mass of dark brown seaweed, no doubt thinking we are utterly and completely bonkers to be out so early on a bitterly cold March morning.

Our boatman rows a steady course towards the island. After seeing the seal, our wholesome Aussie model turns a strange shade of green. With apologies all round she warns that she is about to do a "technicolor yawn" over the side. None of us are feeling great. I guess that's only to be expected after three days and nights on the piss.

We are staying in one of those giant old railway hotels. It's just the kind of place aspiring literary types might lock themselves in and pen the next *Ulysses*; the click-click-click of a muffled typewriter echoing the clipped heels of a waiter delivering yet another round of Guinness.

"Te be sure, it's only a shower." The staff continually say as flood notices are posted. "It'll be fine in de morning."

Thankfully we are all getting on well, bonded by the good god Bacchus. The client's rep turns out to be a pleasant shade of dull, happy to go along with anything and everything provided he has a glass in his hand. Our model has made it abundantly clear in that forthright way Aussie girls have that she is not available for anything other than the photo, but that she might review the situation. The art director and photographer are professional boozers so are perfectly happy to sit it out over Jameson whiskey and the black stuff. After three days we've been assured that the sun will shine tomorrow, Saturday. We have to go for it before our livers wave the big white flag.

So we stagger ashore and make our way up to the Edwardian house on the crest of a hill overlooking the bay. French windows lead from a dining room onto a beautifully manicured lawn and garden, almost exactly as depicted in the layout. The dining room is quickly turned into a bedroom by bringing in a dressing table and placing it at the open windows. Once all the prep work has been done our model has thankfully perked-up. The photographer snaps into action, doing a middle-aged Glaswegian impersonation of David Hemmings in the film *Blow Up*. "That's it darling, hold it there, beautiful you're just oozing natural beauty."

Oozing alcohol is probably more like it!

Before mid-morning, with rain threatening, the shot is well and truly covered. And we have a happy client who has mostly sat quietly in a corner reading a book. We are rowed back to the fishing hamlet of Glengarriff, with its single row of pastel-coloured cottages and an all-purpose pub painted white with a grey slate roof. We are all ravenous and – surprise, surprise – the pub turns out to be the only place that serves a late breakfast.

In that infectious, timeless mist that forms the true spirit of the Emerald Isle, breakfast rolls into lunch... and the end of lunch just so happens to coincide with an important horse race on television... and the publican is also the local bookie so we all place bets... and we win handsomely. So the money goes behind the bar and word soon spreads that "de fillum people have won de big race". And they all come to help us celebrate, and sing and dance and play the fiddle. Pint after pint of Guinness is drunk, but it really doesn't matter. We are in Ireland with our business done...well, almost done.

My client, who I've now been marking for four days, has passed out on the floor. The canny art director directs a photo of him surrounded by empty beer bottles and Guinness mugs and a message to his boss scrawled on a placard and placed on his prostrate body: "Having a great time, wish you were here!" Then, just for good measure, a couple of local girls agree to help out and be a bit naughty in a shot or two: one straddles him, her head with long wild hair thrown back in mock ecstasy; the other feigns the kiss of life. My client is oblivious to it all, snoring away in a blissful stupor. The old-lag art director has his insurance policy, just in case some difficult character we all know doesn't like the photos!

A few hours later I wake up in a haystack with the Aussie model and a wooden shillelagh. I have absolutely no recollection of how we have come to be there let alone where we are in the first place. She sensibly tells me I am far too young for her and suggests I call her kid sister who has just arrived in London and doesn't know a soul. Her name is Olivia and she wants to be a singer.

Later, I lost the phone number and couldn't even remember the surname other than it was yet another double barrel, this time ending in John.

FOURTEEN

Early July 1969

Man is on his way to the moon, the Beatles are squabbling, threatening divorce, Dylan has gone electric, Twiggy has put on weight, drugs are not just addictive but lethal, Brian Jones has drowned in his own swimming pool. The Swinging Sixties are finally winding to a close. I've taken a decision. I'm also on my way. I'm going to follow my dream and see India. But first I'm going to work overseas.

The dispatch boy has delivered a memo; a memo as seminal to me as the one I delivered five years earlier announcing a golf day. As part of the agency's international expansion, it has merged with an Australian company whose head office is in Sydney.

I ask Major Millard if there is any chance of a transfer.

"A ridiculous idea! The place is full of ex-cons and remittance men!"

A few days later I try again, using family reasons – to be with my sister – for wanting to move. In fact my parents are thrilled at the possibility of my going to Australia, and they plan to follow as soon as my father retires. My mother, who was the one who had wanted to come home, now views Australia as some kind of tropical paradise, where she can act as if she were in the cast of *South Pacific*. I don't tell them about the India bit.

This time the major is a little more understanding and arranges for me to be interviewed by the London-based New Zealand account director responsible for the new Australian operation.

"That's a great idea. They could do with some London-trained executives over there as part of the international focus."

After discussion with the Aussie management he tells me there's a job waiting for me on arrival, absolutely guaranteed, and with a good salary. But I've got to get myself there. Fair enough...fair dinkum even. It looks as if I'm on my way. I don't tell a soul, not even Antonia. I hate goodbyes. But there's one "au revoir" I just can't miss.

Hyde Park is filling up. The afternoon is humid, the warm-up acts have done their best – Family, The Battered Ornaments, The Third Ear Band, Screw, King Crimson, Alexis Korner's New Church. What will follow hinges on raw expectation. I'm quite far away from the stage, but not so far that I won't get a good view and a deafening sound is guaranteed. I think of the Ealing Jazz Club of seven years ago. The audience then was no more than 200. Today they are anticipating 200,000 or more. And all for free.

Mick is dressed in white flared trousers and what looks like a white frilly frock from Mr Fish Boutique. He kicks off with a eulogy for Brian. A poem by Shelley is read out, and hundreds of white butterflies are released. Then they rip into *I'm Yours, She's Mine* followed by *Jumping Jack Flash.* As darkness falls Ginger Johnson's African Drummers add a voodoo lash to *Sympathy For the Devil.* I wonder what Australia's equivalent might be. Worryingly, I can only think of Rolf Harris, or perhaps the Seekers.

FIFTEEN

SYDNEY

July 1969

Dawn has broken. I can tell that by a giant sun slowly rising from a red barren landscape. Otherwise I have no idea what time it is. Flight BA 712 has touched-down in Zurich, Rome, Karachi, Calcutta, and Singapore. Finally, I'm in Darwin, Australia, after what seems like a lifetime on a BOAC 707.

I'm feeling seriously rough from lack of sleep, cramp, dehydration – all the signs of loitering jet lag. The thrill of boarding a plane at Heathrow to travel to the other side of the world has been lost in the back-of-plane reality of a small seat, screaming babies and passengers boarding in Karachi who want to cook a meal in the aisle.

Before we are allowed off the plane, two men in shorts walk up the single aisle and spray us with DDT. Everyone is coughing. One elderly German guy seems to think we are being gassed.

I get off as a transit passenger to stretch my legs. They reckon we'll be on the ground for about forty minutes before heading off to Sydney. The combined arrival, departures and transit lounge is a large wooden building, like a barn with a corrugated iron roof and a veranda facing the runway. The white, navy blue and gold livery of British Overseas Airways stands proud at its parking bay, shimmering like a giant cigar tube caught in the early morning rays of a fierce tropical sun. It's very hot, but I'm pleased to say my nausea has passed. I'm getting a second, or possibly a fifth, wind and suddenly feel like celebrating, having a beer in fact, particularly as my mouth tastes like a gorilla's armpit.

A large ceiling fan dominates the lounge, slowly rotating to a loud synchronized click that provides a minimum of air conditioning. What appears to be a plague of flies are working the room, dive-bombing any morsels of food left on the floor. The walls are varnished wood, hung with framed prints of Australian flora and fauna. At the far end I spy a traditional pub bar, complete with brass fittings and a spittoon. Even though it's early morning, a handful of men are sitting at the bar drinking beer from glasses that sport seductive iced condensation.

The men resemble a bunch of overgrown Boy Scouts in tight shorts, long socks and wide-brimmed hats. As I get closer I see that they are all bulky men, a mix of brawn and ruddy-faced boyish looks. They appear to be staring into space. Perhaps they're meditating, or they have been on a night shift and are now treating themselves to a well-earned beer. Maybe they're Austrians rather than Australians, having just arrived from Vienna all wearing the same hiking gear? They certainly aren't from my flight, and I can't see any other planes around.

I order a beer.

"Schooner or midi, mate?"

I point to the large glass in front of the man sitting next to me. Not thinking clearly I hand over an English pound note.

"We don't take pommy money here, mate."

The man sitting next to me suddenly comes to life. "Are you a pom, sport?" He offers his hand. "Welcome to Australia, the finest country on God's earth. The least I can do is shout you a beer. You look fair-dinkum shot."

I thank him, impressed by the hospitality, something my mother is always banging on about.

"No worries mate. So how long are you visiting us for?" Perspiration drips off his face.

My enthusiasm rises as I tell him that I have a job lined-up in Sydney; that I have a sister living up the coast in Newcastle; that I first came to Australia when I was four years old; that I'm really looking forward to living in such a great country. In fact I'm so effusive I'm beginning to sound like a commercial for the Australian Tourist Board.

He eyes me up and down. "Strewth! I shout you a beer and now you tell me you're bloody well moving in. You know what, cobber?" He wags a stubby finger at me. "We don't need poms over here. We're full up, mate. No room at the inn. So why don't you go back home and do something useful, like learn to play cricket!"

Well that came a bit out of left field. Don't know what I did to upset him. He's now ambled off, muttering to himself. The other men are still sitting at the bar staring blankly into space, occasionally wafting away a fly. I take my beer over to the veranda, or observation deck as it is called.

I stare out across what can only be hundreds upon hundreds of miles of red barren landscape, which I know continues beyond the horizon into thousands of more miles. The biggest sun I've ever seen has now settled like a spectacular optical illusion in a vast deep blue sky. Full up are they?

I check into the Sydney YMCA as that's all I can afford. True to form the place is full of creepy-looking characters and smells of stale cabbage and disinfectant. My room is like a prison cell, complete with a solid steel door and peep hole. I think I may even be locked in at night. I unpack my suit and hang it up, can't have it looking creased when I contact Goodwin Advertising.

My plan is to stay at the YMCA until I've taken delivery of my car and can drive up to Newcastle to meet my sister.

I've never actually owned a car so the order I placed from England is a complete indulgence, justified by the fact that it will be ideal for the sunny climate. I cashed in some Premium Bonds and used money left me by an elderly aunt as a deposit. I know I can afford the monthly hire purchase payments based on the salary I've been offered. I suppose an MGB is a bit poseur, but so what. It's not exactly an E-type Jag, the chariot serious poseurs use to cruise up and down the King's Road. Anyway it'll add to the Brit image that I intend to milk for what it's worth, maybe even impress the Aussie birds.

After a massive sleep, I walk down to the harbour for my first glimpse of the famous bridge. The pubs here are called hotels, with green metal canopies stretching out over the pavement. This tends to make them all look the same. Being July, it's mid-winter and fairly cold, although the sky is bright. I'm gasping for a beer so pop into a pub called The Hope. It's a bit basic: an uncarpeted concrete floor, old hospital-style white tiles on the walls and a large circular central bar. The drinkers are all men. I order a schooner of Tooheys and find a pay phone: the secretary to the MD of the agency, a guy called Terence, arranges for me to see him the following day; the car showroom will be happy to see me anytime I care to call by; my sister wants to see me as soon as possible.

"No problems," as the Aussies say.

Time for another schooner. I haven't heard any news since I arrived and wonder how the imminent Apollo 11 moon landing is going. I see an antiquated black and white TV at the far end of the bar. Most of the drinkers have gathered round the set, clearly watching something gripping.

One or two start shouting. "Go, baby go. Yeah, that-a-boy. Man in the moon. You're beaut!"

"So they've got there?" I ask.

"Got where?" The barman replies.

"The moon." I reply.

"Sure did. Twenty-to-one as well. He's a beaut little nag that Man in the Moon!"

Still not knowing news of Apollo 11, I walk down to Circular Quay and look across to the famous bridge, a giant coat hanger holding together two sides of the most beautiful harbour imaginable. Ferry boats that look like bath toys painted green and cream are busy taking commuters from one side of the harbour to the other; yachts are out, in full sail, spinnakers flapping in the breeze. Beneath the bridge, on a finger of land, an opera house is being built to a modern design loosely based upon sails. Moored nearby a replica of Captain Cook's ship, *Endeavour*, can be hired for booze cruises. Strangers pass and take me for granted. And why shouldn't they? All of a sudden I feel desperately lonely, on my own at the other side of the world.

The sun sets on this magnificent panorama giving it a coral-pink hue. The oncoming night air gathers a crisp winter edge that makes me think an overcoat might have been a good idea.

SIXTEEN

The reception area of Goodwin Advertising is more a waiting room with four metal-framed chairs along the wall and a low coffee table scattered with well-thumbed, out-of-date magazines. The area also doubles as the agency switchboard. A frumpy middle-aged lady wearing a pair of large spectacles and too much make-up appears to have the job of receptionist and switchboard operator.

"G'day. Who are you after, then?" She asks as she picks up a telephone hand-set. "Good morning, Goodwin Advertising. Just a minute... I'm putting you through now..."

A metal-ended telephone cord is plugged into its appropriate slot.

"Where did you say you're from? Oh London, that's nice. How's Princess Margaret these days?"

She plugs me into another slot. "There's a young man from London come to visit Terry. Oh, I see. Shall I ask him to call by another time then?"

I don't like the sound of this.

"Oh, to wait. Yes I'll suggest that."

The receptionist turns her flamboyantly framed spectacles on me. "He's a little delayed, but he is aware that you're here."

I take a seat. Most of the magazines are back copies of *Australian Woman's Weekly* with a British Royal on the front cover, except for one with a famous female Aussie Olympic swimmer. I pick up a copy of the *Sydney Morning Herald* only to read that Mick and Marianne Faithfull are due in Australia, as... *"Mr. Jagger"* will be playing the part of Ned Kelly in a new British film about the legendary outlaw. The article goes on to say how inappropriate it is for a pommy pop singer to take such an important role and asks why an Aussie actor isn't cast in the part. Reading further, I find that Mr. Jagger and his girlfriend have an *"unfortunate reputation"*. I guess that the police authorities will be watching them carefully.

Ten minutes pass... then twenty... then half-an-hour and still no sign of Terry, as the receptionist likes to call the managing director. I sit in my best dark blue suit with a light pin-stripe with a Burberry trench-coat neatly folded by my side and know that the vibes aren't quite right in Goodwin Advertising. It's now 12:40, forty minutes after the agreed meeting time. I'm not exactly David Ogilvy, the Brit ad man who took Madison Avenue by storm, but this is poor treatment.

It's a relief when a wiry looking guy wearing a fashionable suit with broad lapels and flared trousers appears in reception.

"G'day, mate." He greets me with an extended hand but no apology. "Paul isn't it? Fancy a beer?"

I correct him on the name and add quick details about the London office and the job.

Terry looks puzzled. "Well let's discuss all that over a jar or two, sport. Tell you what, there's a beaut little diner round the corner. I know you poms don't get to eat much meat so how about I shout you a steak?"

We down a couple of swift schooners in the bar of a business restaurant and Terry, with all the skill of a seasoned ad man, manages to avoid discussing my job. The headwaiter appears to know Terry well and opens a bottle of Penfold's Shiraz as soon as we sit down. The steak is huge and good.

"The finest you'll ever taste, mate." Terry boasts.

A second bottle of Shiraz arrives and I hear about his time living in Earl's Court and how the English Sheilas just couldn't get enough of him; about his homely wife and family; about Aussie league footie and his club in the Northern Suburbs; the problems with the Abos; why Sydney doesn't need an opera house and how the league clubs attract top class singers such as Max Bygraves; how Australian cricket rules the world, led by the achievements of his hero Don Bradman; and, by the end of the second bottle, with a nod and a wink I even get to hear about his extra-marital relationships, including the receptionist-cum-switchboard operator.

He discusses everything but my job, and I know I have to firm things up before a third bottle of Shiraz magically appears.

"So when can I start?"

"Sorry, sport. Don't think I quite get your drift. Start what?"

I talk Terry through the promises I've been given back in London. He shakes his head in disbelief.

"The problem with those stuck-up poms over there is that they don't bloody listen. Yes, I agreed to meet you but that's about far as it went. As it so happens business is a bit crook at the moment and we're laying people off... poor bastards!"

Maybe it's the wine, the isolation, the jet-lag, the pissed off with bull-shitting Aussies, the pissed-off with all this pom stuff, seeing the MGB car and no doubt my deposit disappearing before my very eyes, and spending the rest of my days in the hovel of a YMCA.

"Terry, old sport, do you know what? I'm seriously pissed-off. I've travelled twelve thousand miles to supposedly work for your lousy little, run-down ad agency. I'm not a poor pom, for Christ's sake! I'm an Englishman from one of the finest ad agencies in the world. You should be bloody lucky to have me share a steak with you. And what's more Terry, me old mate, you can fucking well find me a job. Got it?"

Terry pours himself another glass of wine and tops mine up. He extends his hand across the table. This must be the "on yer bike" bit.

I hesitate.

"Go on take it." He says with a grin on his rugged, thin-lipped face. "Do you know what, sport? For a pom you've got balls. I'll see what I can do to help you out. Make a few phone calls."

We go back to his office and within the hour I'm sitting in the ultra-smart reception of the largest American advertising agency in the world.

Although it's not exactly my scene I do recognize the tune: Gilbert and Sullivan, *The Mikado.* It is being sung by my old London pal, Jonathan, as he strides into reception in his shirtsleeves, carrying a couple of ring-bound documents as if he hadn't a care in the world.

"Good Lord!" He asks, "What on earth are you doing here?"

I give him a quick run-down of my situation.

"I've been here a couple of years now." Jonathan says. "Time to move on though, I've just resigned and am heading home."

Then he really raises my hopes. "In point of fact they're after another pom to replace me. The client is eccentric and seems to like us. I think he must have been brought up on Jeeves and Wooster. Anyway he's quite potty."

I point out that I'm actually still feeling drunk after lunch, not the ideal way to go into an interview.

"I wouldn't worry about that." Jonathan assures me. "Most of the agency is half-pissed after lunch. I'm darned sure the MD will have had his fair share!"

Jonathan turns back to his office. "I'll let him know you're here. Put in a good word. Good luck, old chum."

I'm left to enjoy the trendy stainless-steel and smoked-glass furniture and a receptionist who's good-looking enough be a model, even if a bored-stiff one.

The managing director's large corner office overlooks Elizabeth Street at the top end of Sydney's own Hyde Park. On first sight it looks like a cross between a sports changing room and an off-licence: soiled rugby boots and shirts in one corner next to a case of beer and half a dozen cases of wine stacked up against a wall. Documents are piled everywhere.

The MD looks like American tough-man actor Robert Mitchum and, behind a French antique desk, he looks strangely out of place, as if he's just popped in to try it out while the real boss is missing. The small talk is kept to a minimum. I thank him for seeing me at such short notice.

"You're lucky to catch me. Anyway I owe Terry a favour or two."

He takes a few seconds to scan my CV then throws it to one side. "Okay, enough of the pleasantries, tell me mate ... are you any bloody good?"

The fact that I've worked on an international blue chip account seems to impress him.

"Okay, I'm prepared to take a gamble. I'll employ you as an account executive on our top toiletries account, to replace Johnny, who I gather is an old drinking mate of yours. When do you want to get stuck in?"

"How about tomorrow?"

"You're a bit keen aren't you? Unusual for a pom! I tell you what, I'll put you on the payroll from next Monday but I don't want to see you for a couple of weeks as we haven't got an office available."

He selects a handful of documents from a pile next to his desk.

"Here you are. Go to Bondi and have a read of these, useful background provided you're not too distracted by the Sheilas having a winter surf."

The salary I'm offered is better than the one I'd been promised at Goodwin.

As I'm leaving his office, the MD stops me. "Oh, and one other thing I almost forgot. You'll have to take some new fangled psycho test the Yanks insist on. The management here took it when it first came out and the only bloody thing it proved is that we're all over-sexed!"

Jonathan takes me to the local pub, their "other office" to toast my new appointment. The Crown is full of agency people. Quite a few are what the Aussies would call "posh poms", and have the clipped pronunciation of David Niven, or Rex Harrison in *My Fair Lady*. One is even wearing a monocle. Everyone seems to be taking the piss, at the same time as getting completely pissed. The posh poms are unbelievably rude to the Aussies, calling them "convict stock" among other things. The Aussies give it back with a vengeance. And these people work together! No one seems to mind though, provided you buy your round, or "shout" as it's called. There's no need to ask what people want as everyone is drinking beer, except the Brit with the monocle who sticks to dry sherry.

SEVENTEEN

I've opted for ocean blue, far better than primrose yellow, powder blue or white; apart from anything else, I don't want people to think I'm a dry sherry man. The colour is like the Pacific Ocean and goes well with the Connolly black leather upholstery – as sexy as Emma Peel's black leather *Avengers* cat suit.

I remark that Diana Rigg is seriously sexy, but the car salesman has never heard of her.

My first drive is north, up the Pacific Highway, for the long awaited reunion with my sister. I push the shiny new MGB as much as I dare, aware of the advice I'd been given, that the engine needs to be "run in" for a couple of hundred miles. The highway is good and fairly deserted. Towering rock escarpments, rolling hills and eucalyptus trees dot the horizon. I almost expect kangaroos hopping along the roadside, and koala bears hanging from telegraph poles, an aborigine or two blowing a didgeridoo, or throwing boomerangs at passing cars.

The reunion is tearful, sincere, and lasts a few days. My sister gives me guidelines on how to survive, the things the tourist pamphlets never mention: deadly snakes that lurk in the bush; poisonous spiders hidden beneath floorboards; invisible jellyfish that can polish you off in a matter of seconds; currents and rip-tides that can take you off to Fiji before you know it; and of course the sharks.

I return to Sydney and find somewhere to live. It's a bit small, like my flat in Hollywood Road, but at least this time the lavatory is inside. Jonathan had directed me to Double

Bay in the Eastern Suburbs, where he lives. I suppose it's the equivalent to Chelsea in a way: quite chic with smart boutiques and antique shops. The pub where everyone meets is in the centre, on the main road to Rose Bay. It's vast with the usual green metal canopy outside and plenty of wrought iron. The Golden Sheaf is where it all happens on Saturday afternoons, where you sort out the evening party circuit. I think I'm getting on pretty well; it's a bit like being on holiday. Most of the people I come across are ex-pats and Australians who have travelled. The girls are a touch standoffish. They tend to group together, leaving the men to drink beer and talk sport. Sport is an obsession, a religion governed by Australia. Tony Jacklin has just won the Open Golf Championship – the top major – but they don't seem to want to know. There's a lot of chat about sex but I'm not sure how much action. I think getting hammered is the main priority for most guys.

Unfortunately, the account director can't accompany me to my first meeting with my new client. Apparently, he has an important lunch appointment to discuss "new business". I'm told this with a wink and a nudge. The director is a quiet guy who looks more like a bank manager than an ad man, except for the sunglasses. The Brits in the agency say the glasses are a disguise in case his wife's friends see him out on one of his "important lunch dates".

Jonathan tells me that the US "psycho test" ranked the director the most over-sexed man in the agency.

We grab a cab for the ten-minute drive downtown to the client's offices. The modern glass building is in a prime location facing the bridge and next to where the new opera house is being built. It couldn't be more different from my London client who overlooked the Great West Road.

As we wait for the lift to take us up to the top floor meeting room, Jonathan whispers, "Just so that you know, we nickname the two you are about to meet 'Daffers and Biggles'. Not to their faces of course."

I don't get to ask why as the lift door slides open and the client is there, waiting to greet us.

One of them is slight, in his early fifties. The other is much younger and has a magnificent handlebar moustache. We are shown into a conference room with sweeping panoramic views of the harbour, right over to Watson's Bay where there's a beach-side fish restaurant called Doyle's that everyone keeps talking about.

The older man, who must be Daffers, shakes my hand. "And where may I ask were you at school in that fine country that has given us so many poets, in particular William Wordsworth?"

I reel off a few names of the schools I attended, ending with an establishment in Harrow. He's suitably impressed, even if it isn't necessarily the one he has in mind.

The younger man looks like Kenneth More playing Douglas Bader in *Reach for the Sky.*

He lights a pipe. "I must say I prefer Fleming m'self," he says. "That Bond chappie has a hell of a time if you ask me. Reminds me a bit of a fellow I knew in my flying days back in New Zealand."

He takes a few puffs on his pipe, and we become engulfed in clouds of smoke.

Jonathan has a fairly straightforward trade advertisement to present, and it's approved in seconds flat.

Daffers then announces, somewhat theatrically, that he feels a migraine coming on.

"Do you mind, dear boy?" He asks and walks over to a wall, takes his suit jacket off and stands on his head, his body ridged against the wall. I can hear him mumbling something, a recitation.

"I wandered lonely as a cloud that floats on high o'er vales and hills, when all at once I saw a crowd, a host of golden daffodils."

Jonathan whispers, "Told you, didn't I. The old goat's as daft as a brush."

Thankfully, Daffers has his jacket back on in minutes and we head off to lunch. It's a new bistro-style place with a dimly lit basement, but there, secreted away in a corner, is a man wearing dark glasses caressing the hand of an attractive woman across the place settings.

I nudge Jonathan and point out our boss. Too late, the waiter is already leading the client to the next table, and Daffers soon spots him.

"Oh, I say. There's your boss. I thought he had an important meeting?"

"Looks like he has if you ask me!" says Biggles.

Jonathan is quick. "I believe it's with a minister for the interior. We'd better not disturb them. Confidential you know. Shall we have a drink and order?"

Daffers looks as if he's gone into a trance, and then begins to mumble. *"O joy! That in our embers is something that doth live, that nature yet remembers what was so fugitive!"*

Biggles laughs. "I should imagine before the afternoon is out, your boss will be well briefed on the interior!"

We leave them to their confidential discussion. Eventually they leave without finishing their meal.

The agency occupies four floors of a refurbished old building in Elizabeth Street, opposite Mark Foy's department store. It's the second largest ad agency in town and employs around 150 people. On Jonathan's last day a farewell party is planned for the end of the day, but it's likely to start just after lunch. Being new and keen I arrive early to get most of my work done before lunch and the inevitable opening of a few beers — "icy heart starters", as the account men like to call them.

As I get closer to the office, I notice an ambulance parked outside and a couple of police cars. An area of reception has been screened off, and police are checking people into the building from what must be a list of employees. I notice the head of personnel there, looking worried and ask him what's going on.

"A shooting incident," I'm told. "Only got the arm though, otherwise we could have been an art director down."

I'm allowed in the building and told not to linger, to go straight up to my floor.

Nobody is on my floor, and I'm beginning to wonder if there's a gunman on the loose. Someone comes around a corner but it's only the office janitor. I ask him what the hell is going on, he knows all the gossip.

"Laurie, mate. A bit of a player is our Laurie. He's been having it off with this Sheila whose hubbie works nights. He leaves her place early and comes straight into work. All innocent like, even earning brownie points for coming to work early. Anyway, seems as like the hubbie cottoned on and this morning he's waiting for him... and only with a bloody pistol!"

The incident is referred to later in the day at Jonathan's leaving do. My boss naturally has his sunglasses on even though it's almost dark outside.

"I think we should all raise our glasses to Laurie and wish him a speedy recovery." He pauses and takes off his sunglasses for once. "And to think he was only rated number two in that Yankie psycho test!"

The directors get the joke. One points to my boss. "Got yer body armour on have yer, mate?"

He doesn't respond but calls Jonathan forward to receive his leaving gift – a rolled umbrella and an executive briefcase.

"We all know that it never stops raining in pom land so this may come in handy."

It's now sheeting down outside.

"And here's something to keep important things in."

The audience chant, "Open the case!"

Jonathan does so and, to his embarrassment, out fall dozens of packs of condoms.

"Just in case you get lucky, Johnny old mate!" The boss adds as the room collapses into laughter.

EIGHTEEN

January 1970

With summer now well and truly here I've got myself settled in a flat with a couple of other English guys in Woollahra, just behind Double Bay. One of my flatmates has been living here for two years while slowly doing up a terraced house in Paddington, a fairly run-down area closer to town. He seems to think there will be a market for the old villas with elaborate wrought iron balconies on narrow hilly streets. Most of the locals think he's bonkers: yet another pom getting it wrong. He drives an old British Racing Green Jaguar XJ6 which, when parked next to my MGB, makes Greycairn Place, a small cul-de-sac off Edgecliff Road, look like a rally stop. The other guy in the flat has the dubious name of Jules de Beaujolais. He doesn't seem to be around much.

I've come across any number of phony English aristocrats who claim to have titles and estates that clearly don't exist. Their "club" is the beer garden of the Golden Sheaf from Saturday midday onwards. Mad dogs and Englishmen couldn't be truer. I have to say "garden" is stretching it a bit. It's actually an open area paved in concrete flagstones with a solitary palm tree and rusty outside furniture. The specialty of the house is brain sandwiches, which have their own kind of irony as the English mock-toffs munch them down with schooner after schooner of golden amber liquid.

One slightly older toff who prides himself on being an ex-guards officer and having been to Eton, as indeed most of the Brit population of Double Bay claim, has drunk any number of schooners. He's slumped asleep on one of the rusty old garden chairs with washing-line plastic seating. The sun is beating down on his round, red pomegranate face and bald head. At around 4pm a regular occurrence: he suddenly wakes up and stands to attention, saluting.

"Gentlemen it is my duty to inform you," he bellows as if on the parade ground, "that I have had a dream. I have just dreamt that I was having sexual relations with the queen."

One of the older Aussie regulars shouts, "And which queen would that be, mate?" He points to a dandified local antiques dealer, "Billy over there's partial to a bit of shirt-lifting, aren't you Bill me old sport?"

The Guards officer ignores the comment. Still in parade ground mood he picks up an empty beer can. "And now the lesson we've all been waiting for, how to effectively throw a hand grenade."

He proceeds to give a demonstration, using the spent tag as a pin.

"Count to three... HURL!." He does this about four times chucking cans with a straight right arm into the street behind until the beefy no-nonsense landlord throws him out.

"I know the Governor General you know," the toff shouts as he's manhandled into the street. "I think you'll find that by next Saturday you'll be in pokey...where you originally hailed from!"

I'm assured that by next Saturday the routine will start all over again. The dodgy Guards officer is part of the furniture, rusty and odd.

Ridiculous days of unconcern have helped me kiss the sixties goodbye in a land that barely gives a nod or a wink for man walking on the moon or a war in Vietnam. I'm fast getting the hang of the Aussie way of life: it appears to be one long, perpetual holiday, a Freddie Laker packaged tour to Majorca without the sangria but with the laconic line, "She'll be right, mate. No worries!"

My spiritual vision of India is slowly drifting out of my sights like the jet stream of a BOAC VC10. George has given us *Here Comes the Sun*, which has become my new hedonistic anthem along with Bob's *Lay Lady Lay* kicking in when the sun sets.

What the hell! It's not a bad life for a twenty-three year old with still a few wild oats to sow.

Things have taken a slight change on the work front. An American has been transferred in as my account supervisor. I'm fast getting the hang of how much the Aussies resent the Yanks. Pom-bashing is on the whole fun, irritating after a while but nevertheless a game of ribbing for a response. The Yanks, however, are buttoned-down. In the past there have been attempts to bring some New York Americanization into the Sydney office, which the drinking gang proudly dismiss with references to driving the Yanks into a state known as "troppo", as if it were some kind of psychiatric condition.

Troppo is a form of business torture, a manifestation of trying in vain to bring some sense of order to an outfit that operates very efficiently on casualness. The victim eventually snaps, waves a white flag and indulges in booze and associated high-jinks like a man just released from twenty-five years in jail. Such is the personality change that the victim appears to have lost all his marbles, or "gone troppo".

The management of the agency is particularly proud of having written off a previous interloper from the Big Apple who went back in such a wrecked state he lost his senior job in the agency, and ended up driving a yellow cab.

My new intermediate boss is from the Chicago office. He's full of bounce and vigour, very much buttoned-down in his Brooks Brothers button-down shirt, suit trousers just a touch too short and those huge lace-up shoes that Americans like to wear. He seems to thrive on hard work, throwing his bulky frame into everything like a bulldozer.

He called a breakfast meeting for the agency team. Apart from the mail boy and me, no one turned up. And the mail boy only came because he's a keen surfer and is after a transfer to the Hawaii office. The Yank took off his heavy-framed spectacles and rubbed them clean just to ensure he wasn't seeing things as the mail boy put his feet up on his desk and suggested that he take the day off to try his hand at surfing. Without doubt the knives are out for the Yank. He's already alienated the old guard account directors by never dropping by the pub. The Yank has been thrust upon them, no questions asked. The Aussies intend to get the last laugh.

Some good creative people work on the account: Ken is the senior art director who is also getting a bit of a reputation as an artist in his own right. He's recently returned from time spent in the London office and his copywriter partner there has just joined him in Sydney, son of a famous British poet. I don't deal much with them. Instead, the writer I have to work with on cleansing products is the most difficult larrikin character imaginable.

The client has briefed us to prepare names for a new lavatory cleanser. Daffers has made it quite clear that he will fire the agency should the son of one of Britain's finest poets so much as contribute a single word to his lavatory cleanser copy. I've agreed a time schedule with my larrikin writer to see initial ideas with the Yank.

He says, "No worries, mate." Nothing appears. I try again. Nothing. We are now late for client presentation and the Yank is getting seriously twitched. He talks to the copywriter. "No worries." The Yank, being a Yank, takes him literally. And now the first rule of advertising is about to be broken, you could also say the first signs of the illness known as "troppo" are slowly creeping in like a rash between the thighs. The Yank in his frustration fixes a client meeting without actually having seen the work first; a cardinal sin in advertising.

Sunshine is streaming in through the panoramic windows of our client's top floor conference room. The harbour views are breathtaking, hardly the best backdrop to discuss lavatory cleansers. Daffers and Biggles sit opposite us looking expectant. Biggles lights up his pipe. The Yank opens the meeting having first introduced the copywriter who, looking as tight-lipped as ever, places a small leather attaché case on the table in front of him. American flattery flows like the traffic passing over the iconic harbour bridge: "What a great challenge it has been...how it has taken quality time to come up with the right work...how there have been a few false starts but, as always, it is the agency policy to crack it, to get it right... how much the agency honours and respects our important client."

A smug-looking Biggles nods in agreement while Daffers' eyes glaze over. The floor is handed over to the larrikin writer. I have a sense of disaster looming, particularly as we haven't seen anything...yet!

The copywriter carefully unclips the locks on his case. He slowly lifts the lid to let it swing back on its leather straps. The Yank looks decidedly nervous, continuously wiping his brow with a white handkerchief. He's some way from the copywriter so can't see what I have just had the misfortune to see. Should I pretend to faint, to stop the presentation? Daffers enjoys a joke, but this is probably stretching it. From out of the small leather attaché case, a roll of pristine white lavatory paper is produced, handled as if it were some priceless scroll. It is delicately unrolled. In the fatuous manner of a chief barker, the copywriter begins to read names, crude and vulgar names, disgusting names, all spun off lavatory, dunny and shit.

The Yank starts to giggle nervously.

Biggles takes his pipe from his mouth and utters, "I say!"

The Yank pulls it together and asks the copywriter to explain himself.

"Yeah, mate. No worries. A crap brief deserves a crap creative solution!" Whereupon he closes his case and walks out of the meeting.

Daffers goes over to a wall and stands on his head, chanting away about golden daffodils.

Biggles says, "That came a bit out of the sun didn't it?"

I hear the Yank mumble, "I think I need a drink!"

Still in a mild state of shock, as I have to take a share of responsibility for the disaster, I turn my back on the madness and seek solace in the view. Across the beautiful blue water of the harbour, over the frame of an opera house that nobody appears to want, beyond the hunky grey-brick northern support of the famous bridge, I see a giant clown's head with its mouth wide open. Luna Park fairground is open for business.

NINETEEN

A group of us are having an agency April Fools lunch. April 1st was actually a Wednesday, but being conscientious we thought Friday is a better day to disappear from the office for most of the afternoon. Sydney doesn't have many inexpensive restaurants where you can have a meal without risking chronic food poisoning. Our group, mostly Brits who enjoy the April Fool tradition, is eight so the friendly Greek down the road is ideal. A place where you can get stuffed full of vine leaves and Retsina wine for a reasonable price. We tell ridiculous stories of things that have happened to us in advertising, the lavatory roll incident still being the best by far.

Of course it was all a set-up between the sunglass sex addict and Daffers. I wasn't included in the joke as they weren't sure where my loyalties lay. Certain members of the agency were determined to finish the Yank off, to drive him "troppo", and put him in a straight-jacket with a one-way ticket home.

The proper copy had been presented and approved over a lunch involving Daffers and Sunglasses a week earlier.

When the Yank eventually got the gist of the scam he was, understandably, determined to have it out with Sunglasses. I persuaded him not to as he would play right into his enemy's hands. I thought he should be more cunning, to think subtle cricket tactics rather than the slog of baseball. I suggested he buy Sunglasses and some of the other directors in on the act a beer or three and congratulate them on a great joke, which the client really appreciated. Reluctantly he took my advice. It worked. They were completely wrong-footed and had to admit that perhaps he wasn't such "a bad bastard" after all.

As it turned out the Yank got the last laugh. Daffers retired only to be replaced by a young Turk of an Aussie trained in the States. The two can't get enough of each other, with breakfast meetings galore. Sunglasses has moved to handle *Reader's Digest*, and I've been given Lux Beauty Soap as my main responsibility, which makes a pleasant change from floor liquids and lavatory cleansers.

Towards the end of our longish April Fools' lunch, a couple of guys from an adjoining table with no connection to the agency join for a glass or two. Somehow or other the conversation turns to sailing.

"You look like a sailor, mate." One of them says to me. "Fancy a little spin round the harbour this evening?"

I'm instructed to be at a certain jetty in Rushcutters Bay at six o'clock. "Don't be late and bring some grog."

I can't think of a better way to start the weekend than a booze-cruise around the harbour. Maybe there will be a few girls on board?

However, I soon realize there will only be three of us on the 32 ft. sailing yacht. Not to worry, maybe we're going to pick up others somewhere else. There's certainly enough booze for a party, and food. The two guys from lunch don't appear that pleased to see me, and they seem to be taking it all very seriously. Instead of having a beer, I'm ordered to cast off. It's a pleasant evening with a strong breeze but dark threatening clouds appear out over the Pacific. Now I have to admit I'm not much of a sailor, so I'm quite relieved when they start the engine and keep the canvas under wraps.

We cruise up to the harbour bridge, where I'm surprised to see many other yachts gathering, seemingly going around in circles on their motors rather than sail. Most of them are much larger than us. In fact there are a hell of a lot of yachts for a Friday evening, must be thirty or forty and many of them are now winching up sails. I wonder when we are going to pick up the girls?

"Belt up mate. Don't do anything till I tell you."

The other one yells over the roar of the wind. "You have sailed before haven't you? Or do you poms just stick to plastic dinghies in the bath tub?"

My new mates are now winching up the main sail. I've just heard the soft echo of what sounded like a cannon. A plume of white smoke has risen from the direction of the Royal Sydney Yacht Club, and I'm being yelled at to pull ropes I can't find, while the beam of the mainsail nearly decapitates me. Yachts are coming at us from every direction, missing by just a few feet. We're tilted at a steep angle and I'm almost in the harbour, which I happen to know is full of hungry sharks. I've crawled up to the high side. The guy who issued me the invitation is at the wheel, shouting obscenities at everything and everybody. I hope we are only racing as far as Doyle's, that nice fish bar at Watson's Bay?

But we sail past Watson's Bay and are now about to pass through The Heads and into the vast Pacific Ocean. The storm is worsening. Huge waves crash over the bow. The light fades and darkness falls fast.

Okay, good joke when do we head back?

"This is no joke, sport. This is ocean racing."

I have no idea where we are heading; I'm in the hands of two lunatic Aussies I've only just met who seem to have a pathological hatred of poms.

An electrical storm breaks through with monsoon rain and giant waves whipped up by a howling wind.

Some yachts turn back to the safety of the harbour, while we spin like a little cork. Except this cork can sink and we're probably a mile offshore by now, in pitch-black ocean depths. I am terrified. Absolutely bloody terrified. I go down into the cabin to throw up, and pass out.

When I come back up we have passed through the eye of the storm, although the occasional towering wave still catches us by surprise.

"Been a bit crook have yer, sport?"

I groan and ask where we are.

"About two miles offshore, where all the Great Whites like to parade. It's as deep as it gets down there."

The Aussie who invited me on this jaunt nods his head in the direction of the ocean. "Now that you're feeling a bit fresher, there's a small job you can do. I think the navigation light up front is on the blink. Just check it out would you, mate?"

I have to agree or risk being thrown overboard.

I crawl on my stomach using a flimsy rail for support. Water crashes over me as I slowly make my way to the bow, horribly aware of the inky-black ocean depths just inches away. I try not to think of it as I work my way forward: one large wave and I'm a goner, for sure. At least it's not too cold. I finally make it. The light is fine, and I crawl my way back.

"You know what, mate. Next time you go crawling along the deck you might consider slipping into the safety harness. You never know, it could save yer life!"

The charming, friendly skipper then tells me we are in the Bear Island Ocean Race, competing with the likes of the America's Cup yacht, Ragamuffin.

I ask when I can expect to be home.

"At this rate I'd say mid-afternoon Sunday. You haven't got anything planned for the weekend have yer, sport?"

TWENTY

August 1970

I've been in Australia one year and one month. The ocean race joke really shook me up, followed up by an incident when I seriously nearly did drown. A new girlfriend happened to say "Yes" when we were driving along a quiet bit of coastal road. We'd both had a fair amount to drink at a lunch party near Whale Beach. I drove off the road down a barren track to a deserted beach where we re-enacted the classic Burt Lancaster and Deborah Kerr scene in *From Here to Eternity*.

The sun was shining, and I felt on top of the world. I decided to have a quick swim to freshen up before the drive back to Sydney. My girlfriend decided to just paddle. I dived into the surf and swam freestyle out to sea. For a moment, I imagine I'm back in the Med. But when I stop and turn around, I'm surprised to see the shore very far away. I turn to head back but can't move forward. Instead, for all my swimming, I'm drifting further out to sea. My MGB is a small dot, and my girlfriend waves hysterically at me. I know she can't drive and won't be able to fetch help. Anyway, we are miles from anywhere.

It takes me over an hour to swim back to shore, tacking as if I were a yacht. This tactic came to me when I seriously thought I would drown. This feels like my wake-up call. The trouble is I'm not so sure I want to wake up. Maybe I've gone "troppo" without realizing it. Yet there's a faint voice of sanity whispering away at the back of my mind about reality and a place called India… wherever that is.

Lux is the soap of the stars, as the advertising claims, and has been since the twenties when leading actresses such as Myrna Loy and Fay Wray featured in press advertisements. The film star route has continued to this day with big name international actresses starring in TV commercials. Each market area contributes to the cost of the production, according to its size. A good deal for all, you could say – except Australia didn't quite think so. The agency, with the support of the client, has argued that they need to make their own commercial in Australia. There are also some complicated union rules, which I don't completely understand, concerning overseas productions.

The storyline for the Aussie-made Lux Beauty Soap commercial concerns an ingénue American actress, Katherine Crawford – a young Grace Kelly lookalike – enjoying a visit to Australia and all the typical pursuits the country has to offer: the outback, sheep-shearing, sailing, the beach, a sophisticated Sydney garden restaurant. The punch line boasts that Lux soap rejuvenates delicate, photogenic, film star skin and protects it from the harsh Aussie elements.

Eliza's pretty walled garden restaurant in Double Bay is the location for the final shot – a restaurant I've driven past many times but could not afford. The ad will show Katherine enjoying an alfresco lunch with a bunch of "friends". I went to the sheep-shearing shot, not the most enjoyable scene as we were plagued by swarms of flies. I joked with the director and Katherine about the token pom only being allowed to see the flies.

Katherine says, "Oh, that's too bad. Why don't you join us in the restaurant scene?"

So the director has put me in the scene as a dining extra.

I drive to the restaurant and park right outside. I could easily have walked but I'm a film star, they don't walk to location. It's a magnificent Saturday morning in mid-winter, with a deep blue sky and a large sun whose beams make my newly polished ocean blue MGB look as good as it did when I first saw it in the showroom. I'm feeling great, full of anticipation for the day ahead. I'm going to have lunch with a beautiful American actress in a restaurant I've always wanted to dine in, and it's all being filmed. I'll be famous!

The first disappointment is that I'm put on a table some way from Katherine and her "friends", all actors playing bit parts. I'm very much background with a load of grumpy professional extras who don't particularly want to be there.

"Lucky if we get any decent food, mate. And it'll be water instead of wine," says one of my fellow diners as he reads a paperback while waiting for the director to call for the first take.

We are each given a propped plate of cold fish and mixed salad. A wine waiter arrives and fills our eight glasses with clear liquid. I can't help but notice he's used a different bottle for mine.

"Don't get excited, I tell you it's water, mate. Always is," says the diner with the paperback.

I take a sip. Sure as hell tastes like Chardonnay to me. I down the glass and catch the eye of the waiter. He tops me up. I take another sip. The same wine, definitely Chardonnay.

I turn to the girl sitting next to me. "How are you finding the wine?"

"Wine? What wine? If you don't believe me have a taste."

Hers is water. I look over to the director who winks as he gives me a thumbs-up sign before calling "...and...ACTION!"

So far we've had about ten takes; about ten glasses of wine, along with the direction that the background artists should look "jolly".

Jolly? I'm feeling pissed. The rest of the table are stone cold sober, reading books and magazines between takes in the bored way that extras do. The camera set up is changed to cover the shot from the other angle. Another six takes. I've been singled out as the particularly "jolly" one at the table.

"The director really likes the background image of you holding the glass up to toast the table and then downing it in one, as if you are all celebrating something. Okay, got it? Just keep doing that." At least that's what the assistant director has told me.

It's late afternoon, the director has finally called a wrap and I can hardly stand. My table-mates rush off as quickly as they can. Katherine and the director have been chauffeured away as she has to catch a flight back to LA. I'm alone except for the crew packing up their equipment and the young assistant director who thanks me on my "fine performance".

The waiters clear away the mess we've made and lay out settings for their evening bookings. I may as well go home. Or should I pop into the Oakes opposite for a refreshing schooner? I stagger over to the pub and order a schooner. The chilled amber liquid can very often act as a sobering shock to the system. There's nobody around I know. I admire my MGB parked across the road, the black leather upholstery looking as sexy as ever, the bodywork gleaming like a knight's armour in the setting rays of a bold winter sun.

Drink up and drive home. See what's going on; see which party I can go to. I'm in the mood for a good party; it's been a cracking day. I think I'll leave the car at my flat though, I suppose I am a bit pissed.

Two intersections have to be crossed, the second of which has a blind bend. The first crossing is fine, no traffic about. In fact there isn't much traffic around at all. I'm slightly seeing double, yet not when I close one eye. I drive slowly, not taking any risks, and stop at the halt line of the second crossing. Nothing coming. Then I hear a car approaching from my right. I think I can make it. I put my foot on the accelerator. No, not a good idea. Brake. I stop halfway across the road. The oncoming car swerves to miss me but clips my right wing. Shit! The MGB has been dented on one side. The saloon car seems more damaged. The driver gets out, kicking away glass from his broken headlight. My eyes hit on the yellow *For Hire* sign on the roof of the blue and white saloon. I've hit a cab.

I'm too numb to get out of my car. I sit, my hands frozen on the steering wheel, gear in neutral, engine ticking over, my foot still on the brake. I imagine the police turning up at any moment. The burly cab driver shakes his head in disbelief and strides over to my open topped-car, his fist is clenched as if ready to swing a punch. "You little bastard..."

I throw the car into reverse just as the punch heads my way. The cab driver steadies himself on the bonnet then slides to the ground as I reverse. Suddenly I'm sober, as sober as a judge. The cabbie gets to his feet and runs toward me. I speed off leaving an ominous threat echoing in my ears.

"I've got your number you little bastard. We'll track you down. There'll be no bloody escape, mate!"

Sydney taxi drivers are known as a law unto themselves; a fraternity not dissimilar to the Mafia. And now I presumably have a few hundred of them after my hide.

My flat-mate, the one with the XJ6, knows a dodgy lock-up and repair garage. I quickly dump the MGB there with instructions to patch it up, and sell it as quickly as possible. I agree to split the price with the garage, which will leave me enough to pay off the hire purchase.

It's now close to midnight. I walk down to the jetty in Double Bay along the wooden planks to the end. The metallic tinkle of yachts' rigging reminds me of something. I sit on the end looking out over the harbour at the twinkling lights of dwellings that have not yet gone to sleep. There seems to be a party going on in a house overlooking the bay. I can hear laughter, the distant sounds of *Abbey Road*. I wish I were at the party, chatting up some hot bird. No I don't. I've had enough. The crash has finally brought me to my senses. Do I really want to idle away the rest of my life in a state of permanent, ignorant holiday mood? I suddenly get what the ting-ting of the rigging sounds like: the finger symbols of Hari Krishna.

THE HIPPY TRAIL

CALCUTTA

Early September 1970

Bodies are laid out in neat rows, covered in blankets and lining the road. More are in trees. They stretch out along lower branches, like giant cats. The smell is sewer mixed with pungent joss stick. It's misty and humid. A cow has appeared from the ghostly dawn light. It bows its head to drink stale water from a giant pothole.

I stare out the window of the VW Kombi as we head to Dum Dum airport. An elderly American couple are the only other passengers. They struggle to capture the scene with their expensive camera. I don't possess a camera; I'll rely on the pictures in my mind.

On a distant horizon a huge slice of orange peeps up from a barren landscape. As if from the bowels of a stage, it slowly rises and grows into a giant blood-orange sun. Its rays illuminate the road, and bodies rise and stagger forward like zombies. Vividly coloured saris drift into view: green, red, blue and turquoise, purple, ochre. Some of the men amble to a sewer to urinate, others squat and defecate.

The minibus driver leans across to me, and whispers, "Say good morning to Calcutta, city of joy and sorrow."

Actually I can say goodbye to Calcutta as I'm heading for Kathmandu. The flight from Sydney was delayed, so Qantas put me up in an old colonial hotel, The Grand, in the centre of town. I have an open ticket, Sydney to Delhi via Kathmandu, and that's it. I plan to travel overland back to London. A vague plan to hitch and use public transport plays in my head. I've also picked up a leaflet for an overland bus leaving Delhi in a few weeks. I'm a free agent, travelling solo with no one else to worry about.

Despite the dawn, the humidity is getting to me. I pull a giant-sized workman's handkerchief out of my jeans pocket and wipe my brow. I check my documents are in the button-down chest pocket of the bus driver's shirt I bought in Sydney, just the job for the rigours of travelling. For some reason I think of the MGB, worlds away from the chaos unfolding before me. I wonder if the guy who bought it got his lights punched out by an irate cab driver. I do feel bad about that.

We've hit rush hour on the road to Dum Dum: battered vehicles move like dodgem cars, swerving at the last minute to avoid a head-on collision; a few ancient bullock carts plod past, steersmen wrapped in biblical robes shout abuse as twentieth century vehicles cut them up; swarms of rickety Hero bicycles, each one with a ting-a-ling bell, try to establish their presence on a road that has no markings other than potholes; Royal Enfield motorcycles drive cautiously with a sari-clad girl or two perched side-saddle; tiny three-wheel tuk-tuk taxis skilfully manoeuvre through the mayhem; commuter buses, stuffed full of passengers, with more sitting on the roof. Holy cows amble through as they evidently have the divine right of way. Holy cow indeed! I've never seen anything quite like this.

The airport check-in desk has a large old-fashioned weighing machine. We stand on it with our luggage. I don't weigh much as I have only a holdall with *Dunlop Golf* on the side. Its contents are meagre, a few extra clothes and a toothbrush and paste. My sleeping bag is standard camping issue.

I'm booked to travel on a Royal Nepal Airlines flight to Kathmandu. The departure lounge is spacious but faded, with rows of fixed plastic bucket seats and a decrepit ceiling fan. A large map of the Himalayas decorates a wall and shows the flight route with notable mountain peaks marked with their height.

Everest, that's the one I want to see. Perhaps we'll fly close enough to get a peek. I'm now waking up after the long haul from Sydney and feel incredibly excited, more so than I can ever remember. I'm beginning a journey, which will lead eventually to London, but I'm not sure how or when.

A slogan runs above the map: *Royal Nepalese Airlines – The Regal Way to Go!* The *'o'* of Royal has a little crown above it. I chuckle at the irony hidden within the message.

A man wearing a loincloth sits next to me. His hair is platted into dreadlocks and a beard covers most of his face. I can't help but notice that a blue, yellow and pink pattern has been painted on his dusty body. I assume he must be a holy man, or sadhu.

"Don't laugh, man," he says. "It may be your turn next. Zey are always loozing planes up zere. Never reported. Never happened."

His pronunciation doesn't sound particularly Indian, let alone holy. I ask him where he's from.

"In which life?" He says.

I suggest the current one.

"Hamburg, I guess," he says through his mass of facial hair.

The crew have difficulty getting the door closed. Nobody is wearing an identifiable uniform and they all seem to be constantly arguing. Four have squeezed into the tiny cockpit, with a graceful stewardess in a sari left to keep an eye on us. The plane is a twin-prop Dakota, three to a single canvas seat with one long safety belt stretched across us. There are about twenty passengers. The German hippy holy man is sitting behind me. I've managed to get a window seat, a cloudy view out of a small Perspex aperture.

I ask the hippy if we are likely to see Everest.

"It's called Jomolangma." He shouts in my ear above the din of the propellers. "And Jomo Miyo Lang Sangma is ze name of ze resident female deity. She is orange and bright-looking and rides a red tiger. She wears a garland of many kinds of flowers around her head and robes of many colours. In her right hand iz a long bowl of food and in her left hand a mongoose that spits wealth. A cool chick, ja?"

We're in the air for about half an hour before we begin to descend, not as in crashing, more landing. I must say I haven't seen any mountains yet. I look out of the window and I swear I can see an airport. It looks familiar. In fact it looks just like Dum Dum. The plane taxis to a halt at the identical spot it was parked in 45 minutes earlier.

I ask the German if he knows what the hell is going on?

"Who knows, man? Maybe zey change zair mind?"

We receive no announcement, and no one seems concerned, except me. The crew tumbles out of the cockpit still arguing. I look out the window and see a small Shell tanker heading towards us. Steps have been wheeled up to the door and the crew get off. The lady sitting next to me translates the Hindi announcement for me, and I learn that we are to remain seated. One or two of the crew light cigarettes as the tanker attaches its hose to the plane's fuel connection.

The lady next to me states the obvious. "Not enough petrol it would appear!"

The hippy leans forward and says full of clipped sarcasm, "Zey usually figure zat out when itz too late, in ze middle of ze Himalayas...Ze regal way to go, Ja?"

Kathmandu

The very name conjures up mystique, ancient riddles with green-eyed idols, legends and exotic dreams. The smell is cow dung and aviation fuel.

I push my way through a crowded airport shed that is full of anxious-looking Indians and Nepalese; some appear to have all their worldly possessions bundled up for check-in, others scurry along like commuters in London Underground during rush hour. Apart from my plane, there don't appear to be any other flights, but this doesn't seem to deter the crowd. I'm only sorry that I didn't get to see Everest. There again maybe I did – all the peaks look the same at 30,000 ft.

After I change some money at an official kiosk, I say farewell to the German sadhu who is off to a temple up in the foothills.

"Namaste, man. Watch out for ze hippies, zey can be real tiring."

I wonder what he does for money? I've got about $300 in travellers' cheques to see me through, which I keep safely zipped up in a money belt.

On the German's advice, I grab a bicycle rickshaw taxi. The driver is a friendly guy, who peddles like crazy while I loll in his bamboo chariot. In between ringing his bicycle bell, playing chicken with huge lorries and swerving to avoid the odd cow and numerous potholes, he chats away.

"You from rich country?... You want nice, swanky hotel?"

I try to assure him that I'm not rich, that I'm a student seeking cheap accommodation. I can't wait for my beard to grow and look a bit more the part.

"You hippy? You want hashish? Very good price if you buy from me."

I decline the offer, impressed by how he can peddle while trying to do a deal at the same time.

"You want pretty girl to show you around? My sister very pretty. She show you good time."

I say no, thanking him all the same and ask him to drop me where the hippies hang out as I think I'll find cheap accommodation in their district.

After about half an hour he stops in what he calls "Freak Street" and charges me a pittance for the ride.

The Summer of Love has decamped from California. Everywhere there are bands of hippies in local clothes, marigolds galore, Afghan waistcoats and beads. I ask a seated hippy for pointers on where I might find somewhere to stay. He's English and nods in the direction of a teahouse, his eyes completely vacant as if he's in a trance.

The teahouse is like a chapel meeting with rows of hippies sitting cross-legged on the floor, while others are sprawled on cushions at the back of the room. The place reeks of sweet marijuana. Everyone seems to be smoking a joint as music from The Doors flows out of large army surplus amps placed high on a shelf. Jim Morrison is groaning about it being the end.

A stoned American shouts out that it's too depressing. "Let's hear the Stones, man."

A few minutes later *Paint it Black* echoes around the room. It's good to hear Mick and the boys again. A hippy and an angelic-looking girl draped in daisy chains and marigolds begin to dance, slowly gyrating like mime artists.

The girl waves her unkempt long blonde locks around like a silken whip in time to Keith's guitar riffs. Somehow I don't think I'm going to find accommodation here.

Another hippy tells me to head off to Durbar Square. "All life meets there, man."

I walk the short distance to Durbar Square stunned by the shambolic beauty of Kathmandu. I feel I've hitched a ride on H G Wells' *Time Machine*, turned the dial back a few centuries and ended up in Elizabethan days. As if to prove the point someone hurls a bucket-load of garbage out the top floor window of a wooden, medieval dwelling. A group of ravenous-looking dogs attack it and a chicken flutters off. The alleyways are desperately narrow and full of people, many carrying bulging bundles or brass jugs, presumably full of liquid, perilously balanced on their heads. It's crazy, but I like it. Beautiful kids run riot, throwing what appear to be mud pies at each other, or maybe it's cow dung.

Durbar Square comes as a relief from the claustrophobia of medieval alleys. Luckily it's not too hot as we are 4,500 ft. above sea level. I have a tin army-surplus water flask, which I keep topped up and drop water purification tablets into, even though they leave a musty taste.

My previous experience of a square is St James's with its manicured inner garden and a giant bronze statue of an English king on a horse. But this one is stuffed full of huge pagoda-style temples on high stone steps. The hippies are sprawled on the steps taking in the sun and smoking the inevitable dope. The colours of the temples are vivid with red brick, dark carved wood, white, red and gold painted canopies. The hippies look pallid by comparison.

It's late afternoon and I need to find somewhere to stay. I approach a reasonably clean-cut hippy, most of his body hair sprouting from a lush Viva Zapata moustache.

He's American and a little older than the rest.

"Can you recommend somewhere inexpensive for me to stay the night here in Kathmandu?"

"Do you know Paris?" He asks, before continuing. "There I was innocently walking along Avenue Saint Honoré when this stiletto falls from the skies. Misses me by inches. Impales itself in the wooden bench I'm about to sit on. I know it's the CIA by the cut of the blade. They're here as well, buddy. Watch out, particularly if you know Paris."

The American offers me a roll-up joint, which I feel obliged to take, coughing on the first drag. I ask again about accommodation.

"Do you know the Greek Isles? There I was innocently having a nap on a deserted beach. I've taken my togs off as there's nobody in sight, lying face down in the sand. Sure I fell asleep, wouldn't you? Anyway, I'm woken up by these guys singing *'Oh what a beautiful morning'* from *Oklahoma.* They've formed a circle around me, and they're all bollock naked! I tell you, I'm out of there like a shot, swimming out towards a yacht moored in the bay. A Chinese chick helps me on board and gives me a towel, offers me opium. Have you ever tried Chinese?"

The tunnel into the Grand Central Lodge is linked to the Library of Transcendental Meditation and follows a ten-yard-long sewer opening into a small sunny courtyard. The fantasist American eventually gave me the address. I asked where he was staying, if only to avoid him. He answered, "Saigon, but not just at the moment."

The proprietor is a happy-faced Nepalese man dressed like a hippy. He shows me a tiny stone-floored room with an ancient, mouldy mattresses lying in the centre. For some reason I lift it up with my foot. A rat as big a squirrel scurries away.

"Did you see that rat?" I ask.

"Are you suggesting we have rats, sir? The Grand Central Lodge is the cleanest of establishments. You will never see a rat in my house."

I explore temples and villages in the towering presence of the mighty Himalaya foothills, dark green and omnipresent with the razor sharp peaks of the monumental mountain range occasionally showing through cloud, like a cutthroat beneath a cloak.

In the nearby village of Patan I catch a ceremony that involves painting cows in bright colours and festooning them with flowers. Dancers in face masks parade before them and hold huge umbrellas over heads and horns, presumably to protect the cows from the sun. Or rain, as it comes in monsoon proportions, mostly in the afternoon. I slosh about in rubber sandals made out of old car tyres – Firestone, I think!

I make a trip to the monkey temple. As the name suggests, it's full of sacred monkeys swinging everywhere. Animals seem to have a pretty good time here.

Time has become meaningless. Not because of drugs. I'm not on the stuff unless pushed. I think it's just the timelessness of the place, the *Time Machine* on pause. I haven't spoken sensibly to anyone since I arrived. And I can't remember how long ago that was – five days, a week?

I have one meal a day in the evening, with fresh fruit and milk from a local dairy during the day. Thankfully I've not yet been ill, except for tooth-ache cropping up and I feel I ought to visit a dentist, just in case.

I ask the hotel proprietor for a recommendation.

"You want expensive or reasonable price?" He asks.

I most definitely want inexpensive.

"Oh, then the *Happy Smiles Clinic* will sort you out," he replies, flashing a row of immaculate white teeth. He directs me along a few alleys, turn right at one of the temples and the clinic will be right in front of me.

Sure enough *Happy Smiles* is there, sandwiched between a hardware store and a place selling herbs and spices with goods laid out on long wooden shelves.

The dentist has his chair, an old dining room carver bolted to a shelf. The patient is secured to the arms with leather straps while the dentist drills into his open gob using a drill powered by a young boy peddling furiously on a stationary bicycle. This power source is thoughtfully placed behind the patient, whose legs kick out in agony. Not surprisingly my toothache miraculously disappears.

Benares

I need to move on. I want to get to Delhi, particularly as there's talk of problems with Air India. I pay my bill at the Grand Central Lodge – three dollars – and take a rickshaw bicycle to the airport.

It's chaos there. The problem appears to be overbooking. The road to India has been closed due to the monsoon, so everyone is trying to fly out. American and French tourists are particularly irate as they have to catch connecting flights in Delhi. The best I'm offered is a confirmed seat leaving in one week, but instinct tells me this could be two or even three weeks unless I slip someone a few significant notes, which of course I'm not going to do. I'm just another penniless western hippy, the bottom of the list compared to rich tourists.

Pissed-off and worried I could end up like the others in Freak Street, I leave the cattle-market of a departure area and wander outside. An American, dressed in a cream coloured silk kaftan and looking rather like the pianist Liberace, is gathering a small crowd of tourists around him.

He catches my eye. "Hey you, young man. Where are you trying to get to?"

I run over and tell him.

"Okay, you're in if you want. Have you got a ticket?"

I produce it from my pocket and offer it to him.

"No, not me. Give it to Rajiv over there. He's in charge of tickets."

Rajiv is a handsome Indian guy of about my age, immaculately dressed.

I ask him what's going on. "My boss has hired a jet. It only seats thirty." Then he adds in a snide way, "So you're lucky to have caught his eye."

Here we go again I think. After only about half-an-hour the jet begins to descend. Surely we can't have reached Delhi already?

I ask an elderly American sitting next to me.

"Delhi? Who said we were going to Delhi? This is Benares, but at least it's India. We should be able to get connecting flights to Delhi from here quite easily."

I have no idea where or what Benares is and ask my fellow passenger.

"You know how Mark Twain described the place?" He replies in a professorial way, pleased that I've asked the question. "Older than history, older than tradition, older even than legend, and looks twice as old as all of them put together."

Mr. Twain wasn't wrong. He might also have added that Benares is the top spot in India for cremations. I've never actually seen a corpse before and feel a bit of a shock when one is carried onto the Benares airport bus I take into town. Okay it is wrapped in what looks like an old carpet and I think it travels free.

I check into another inexpensive guesthouse while I consider how the hell I get myself to Delhi now Rajiv and Liberace have disappeared with my air ticket. Looking on the map it seems a hell of a long way.

"If you could sail there, that's what I would most definitely recommend. Oh yes, the navy is in my blood you know."

I'm staying at the Prakash Hotel with "grey atmosphere and flash latrins". My "latrin" isn't at all flash – just a hole in the ground in the corner of the cement-floored room, next to a dilapidated shower that only runs cold water, which is just as well as Benares is unbearably hot.

Mr. Mukherjee the proprietor has festooned the place with black and white framed photos of destroyers and frigates. He bores me over breakfast of cold toast and marmalade as he talks of his days in the Indian Navy.

I get out as quickly as I can and walk the heaving, filthy streets of Benares dodging cows, camels and beggars. My stubble is itching like crazy, having reached that pre-beard stage. But I don't have a razor.

It's easy to see that there aren't so many hippies in Benares, just thousands of locals and visitors trailing their deceased loved ones.

I've been persuaded to see the burning grounds by one of the hundred or so Indians who endlessly pester me with offers.

"A most enjoyable boat ride," as one boat owner puts it. I decide to please my old sailor guesthouse proprietor by telling him I've taken to the water, sailing the holy River Ganges.

The craft is little more than a rowing boat. The oarsman isn't the guy I've paid a few rupees to, but a bearded local wearing only a loin-cloth. He also wants a payment, albeit the equivalent of a few pence.

His English is good. He rows out into the middle of the Ganges, which is a rich, murky mud colour. So far I've seen two dead dogs float by on the strong current, one horribly bloated. The sun is blisteringly hot, and I'm beginning to feel sick. My bowels aren't too good either despite the medicine I've been taking (recommended by the Indian navy). We have to travel some way down river to reach the cremation site.

My oarsman is a good guide: *Benares is the city where Hindus flock for purification and death and to be touched by the divine light that glows from a thousand temples, gathered along the holy river Ganges. Washing in the sacred waters will cleanse away all sin. To die next to the river and have one's ashes scattered into the water is the ultimate goal of every devout Hindu, it releases the soul from the eternal cycle of birth and rebirth.*

There's an Indian guy standing on the bank wearing a beautiful flower print dress. He's tall and his hair has been tied up to give it a bouffant look. His eyes are heavy with kohl and he's gesticulating to the river, willing it to pay attention, singing a song I can't hear. Ridiculous I know, but I'm reminded of Dusty Springfield. Possibly to take my mind off sickness and the bowel issue I start to sing, "*You don't have to say you love me.*"

I deliberately get the words wrong. This isn't meant to be disrespectful. Maybe I'm hallucinating, as it is unbearably hot.

My guide likes the song. "We sing to death in India. And you also?"

The bodies are lined up wrapped in coloured cloths and covered in flowers as they wait to be cremated on one of a number of roaring pyres. Flies are everywhere, particularly around the bodies, and the relatives as they wail, and the half-naked people immersing themselves into the river. The crackle of burning wood and golden red flames make the temperature twice as hot. It is humbling. I think of somewhere unmentionable on holy waters, almost unthinkable in the circumstances: the divine tragedy of hell on earth. I need to sing again, it helps release the emotion.

I'm beginning to get a bit fed up with this hippy trail business and I desperately want to get to Delhi to sort out some civilized transport home. The leaflet I picked up for PBK Tours talks of a "luxury coach". That sounds more the thing, and they're English so it should be reliable. I just hope I can afford the fare, although someone along the line said it was only about fifty quid, Delhi to Victoria Coach Station in London. That doesn't sound much for a luxury coach.

I leave after three days in Benares. I can't take any more. The proprietor eventually suggested I take a train to Delhi.

"An express service. Very fine comfort. Not as good as by sea though."

I buy a third-class ticket, being cautious with my limited funds. The train is long, maybe as many as fifty or sixty carriages long. And like everything else in the subcontinent it's packed to the rafters with people. The travel is slow and creaking as the railway stock is old. Snail is more suitable than "Express". The third class compartments could be cattle carts, and I actually wonder if I'm in fourth class. Bodies are squashed everywhere, including in the luggage rack. Other passengers eye me with a calm, impassive air of contempt for being the only westerner in their space. This time I will say it: I've bought a single ticket to Hades, a theme park ride through a Hieronymus Bosch painting.

When we lurch into a station, the demons really come into their own: pitiful beggars deformed in the most unimaginable ways crawling along the platform imploring me to show some mercy, to throw a few rupees their way. Some are without limbs and have iron castors screwed into their rotten flesh to help them speed along and beat their fellow beggars to a possible drop of alms. I see lepers expose their putrid, diseased bodies to give the act of begging some credibility. A man with elephantiasis and what looks like two heads pushes a young child along in a crude wooden pram.

When night falls, track-side brazier fires give the canvas an added tinge of hideous reality. Demons of the night: ghastly, deformed apparitions lurking in the shadows. They can't help it. They are just hoping to return one day as something better.

Show some compassion, think how lucky you are, I tell myself over hot sweet tea bought from an opportunistic vendor whenever we shudder to a halt in a country station. Mainly, I drink bottled water and wait for it to inflame my stomach. I begin to wish I had a travelling companion, someone I could share the experience with, and who might help me believe that it isn't all a living nightmare.

Delhi

"So where the bloody hell have you been?" The white sari, pale skin and long natural blonde hair make her appear like some kind of virginal spectre amongst the crowd of business men and women in the large, dark-wood furnished café – Delhi's equivalent of a Joe Lyons Corner House.

The question, tinged with a touch of fury, is very much aimed at me.

"For the past week I've been coming to this lousy coffee house at the agreed time of 11am and no show. You can count yourself lucky as this was to be the last time I ever intended to wait again for an unreliable pommy bastard."

I'm in Connaught Place, New Delhi, and have wandered into the cleanest and largest coffee house I could find for a cup of sweet Indian tea. There again, perhaps there is more to it than just the need for tea, perhaps something subliminal is jolting my muddled mind?

The agency leaving party...of course! As I make my way over to Kerry's table it all comes flooding back. The agency let me leave almost straight away after I told a small fib about a family illness back home. They even threw a party for me. That was when Kerry told me she was stopping off in Delhi on her way to England, and eventually on to Ireland to stay with a relation who was something to do with the movie business. We discovered our dates overlapped and agreed to meet in the largest coffee house we could find in the largest, most famous square, in New Delhi on such and such a day.

I sit down at her table and stare into her ice-blue, pissed-off eyes. I have a good excuse with the Benares diversion. Kerry looks tremendous, one of the most-fancied girls in the agency. Not that I ever got to take her out.

A few teas later, having explained that I'm sharing a room with five others and a dozen cockroaches, her ice melts.

"You can't possibly camp out with a whole load of bloody hippies."

She offers me the spare bed in her room in a cheap hotel in Old Delhi. "You can pay your share, and no trying it on."

I go and collect my things, and we grab a tuk-tuk.

We are dropped at the start of the smallest alleyway imaginable, too narrow for even a tuk-tuk. Kerry, who clearly likes to take charge, pays the driver a few rupees taken from her embroidered shoulder bag. We walk down myriad alleys, shouldering our way through the crowds and past the occasional cow. The route is like a maze with the constant babble of people, distant traffic and occasional flute music, making me think of snake charmers. I feel I will need a trail of string to ever to find my way out again. Eventually we reach our destination: *Malabar Hotel – House of Comforts*.

The room is a lean-to on the roof with an open shower in the corner. You have to go down a floor for the communal lavatory, and I can't imagine what that's like. Two metal-framed beds are next to each other with well-worn, once-white sheets on them.

"That one's yours. Do you want a shower?"

I do seriously need a shower but suddenly feel self-conscious.

"Don't worry about me, just get your togs off and clean up. I've even got soap. Sorry it's not Lux Beauty Soap!"

Kerry sprawls out on her bed and casually reads a book as I strip off and soap up in cold water. She suddenly bursts out laughing. "Don't worry, I'm not laughing at you. It's the book."

Kerry shows me Old Delhi. Having been here for over a week, she knows the places to see that are off the beaten track. We stop for a meal at a rooftop restaurant where she knows the owner. Dusk is falling. Children are flying kites but, being high up, all we see are the paper images of dragons or fierce masks swooping and swirling in the hazy pink sky like swallows in the breeze.

"The owner is a friend of my dad and gives me free meals every now and then," Kerry explains as I anxiously look at the prices.

The owner is a gregarious, small, round man who confirmed this.

"Tonight it is, how you say?...on the house. And do have some Indian beer. A friend of Kerry's is a friend of mine, particularly an Englishman."

After the meal and a number of ice cold, strong beers, we stroll down Chandni Chowk, the main drag running through Old Delhi. I'm feeling quite drunk, not having touched booze for a couple of weeks. Kerry is definitely tipsy, giggling away at everything and anything. Coloured lights and neon signs flicker giving everything a fairground effect. The crowds seem more intense than ever, vying with the erratic flow of eternal traffic for command of the road. Does Old Delhi ever sleep? We aren't far from the Red Fort, almost at the street opposite India's largest mosque, the Jama Masjid with its tapering minarets and onion domes. I slip my arm around Kerry's slim waist, partly to guide her and more as a sign of interest for later on. She doesn't object despite her initial warning not to try anything.

Unlike life in Sydney where it was a number one priority, sex isn't top of my mind during this marathon journey. In many ways the mere thought of it is kind of hypocritical when set against the pitiful sights of humanity that crawl and beg before you.

Yet after a few beers, and Kerry looking like a tall blonde goddess...

Of course she's being pestered by local jack-the-lads: "Hey missy, you a film star? You want me show you swanky night club? You want to buy happy pills? Really good price for you. Do you know the Beatles?"

A pleasant-looking young man in grey trousers, white shirt and wearing glasses sidles up to us and begins to tell us the history of Chandni Chowk: *Laid out in 1648 by Shah Jehan's daughter with a central canal flanked by merchants and noblemen's mansions.*

We thank him and explain that we don't need a tour guide. He understands and then, ever so politely, asks Kerry if she would do him a big favour.

He produces a pencil and paper saying that he wants to write to his girlfriend in England but doesn't know the correct words for various things he wants to say.

"You write it down please, missy, if I tell you what I want."

Kerry agrees. The noise of traffic and a cacophony of ringing bicycle bells make it difficult to hear what he's dictating so Kerry bends down for him to whisper into her ear.

As if caught by an electric shock, she suddenly straightens and whacks him around the head. "Piss off, you filthy little sod!"

He scampers away into the all-enveloping chaos of Old Delhi.

At least I wasn't whacked around the head. I mean come on! What else am I supposed to do? I take a shower and lie on the bed to dry off. She takes a shower naked in front of me. Then lies naked next to me. I place my hand on her breast...

Anyway, I'm soon in the YMCA in New Delhi, virtually back where I started, and the beautiful Kerry has caught a flight to Athens to check out the Greek islands. The other reason I'm in the modern and fairly expensive YMCA complex is to make contact with PBK Tours, as this is their unofficial operating office and ticket desk.

"It was found on earlier trips that the main objective of the majority of applicants was to get to and from India as cheaply as possible. After experience with various vehicles,

a bus proved the most suitable – a 41 seat Leyland Luxury Coach."

So reads out the lank young Englishman who is MD and principal driver for PBK Tours. He's seated at a school desk in the entrance hall of the YMCA and sells his trip from a cheap black and white leaflet.

Quite a few students and hippies listen to him. "The journey time, of course, depends on how we fare."

I'm not altogether sure what he's getting at as we're not exactly depending on winds and tides to speed us along. A guy standing next to me notices my apprehension and tells me to expect about 4 weeks.

Then the driver adds as a throwaway line, "I have to say that there are probably more comfortable and undoubtedly more expensive ways of travelling. Facilities and conditions on route are bad by our standards, and sleeping accommodation will require a certain amount of roughing it. This trip therefore is more suited to the younger age groups. It should be treated as an expedition rather than a tour."

I join the queue and buy a ticket. He accepts US dollar traveller's cheques, and the equivalent in pounds sterling is a little under fifty quid.

The next person to buy a ticket can't be a day under fifty. He has a distinctly military air about him in his baggy khaki shorts and army shirt. Behind him are a group of six hippies in their mid-twenties: four men and two girls dressed in quintessentially Indian and Nepalese gear. One carries a large sitar. The women look pretty emaciated, made more garish with their henna-dyed hair – one purple, the other orange. From their accents I'd say they are Scandinavian, possibly Danish. I ask where the bus is parked and the driver tells me just around the corner.

"But you can't board until we leave in two days' time. Meanwhile you'd better get all your visas sorted out."

I'm handed a visa checklist. Most of them I got in Sydney. A couple I'll need to get tomorrow from the embassies in New Delhi.

The bus looks like the coach from the Beatles, film *Magical Mystery Tour*, which may well be why the hippies like to call it the "Magic Bus". But I'm pleased to see it has extra-wide tough-looking tyres. It doesn't exactly fit the description of luxury, and it has a six thousand mile journey ahead of it over some of the roughest roads imaginable.

I feel a sense of exhilaration, an adventure not to be missed. I'm sorry Kerry wasn't up for it, preferring the easy "fly me" option. There again I'm not sure I could have coped with all her naked prick teasing, and telling me to "piss off" whenever I made a pass.

The Khyber Pass is probably best seen single.

Khyber Pass

Thirty of us are on board as we depart from the YMCA. A group of kids have gathered to see us off, making one last attempt to beg sweets or money. They've got the wrong crowd; the most they can expect from this penniless bunch is a *Bic* biro. The kids chase us down the road yelling, waving, screaming with excitement on our behalf, India's version of Australians casting coloured paper streamers to departing ocean liners, the final snap is the break of bonds.

The hippies occupy the rear of the coach, together with rucksacks and sleeping bags too large to put in the overhead luggage rack. The guy with the sitar has already taken up a crossed-leg position plucking away like a poor-man's Ravi Shankar. I've taken an aisle seat so I can stretch out my legs. A small English girl with short mousey hair and a strong Birmingham accent asks if she can have the window seat. She's a student, not in the least bit hippy. The middle-aged army man takes the seat directly behind me and immediately introduces himself to everyone around. He's Alf from Nottingham and has been retracing his army days in India. My seat companion has buried her nose in a well-worn copy of Tolkien's *Lord of the Rings*. I've noticed a number of hippies reading it as if it were some kind of bible. I've got Norman Mailer's *The Naked and the Dead*; I think it's a touch more realistic.

We've been travelling for a few hours and already there have been a few roadside loo stops. The plan is to get to Lahore by nightfall and then push on to the Khyber Pass. The countryside is flat and dusty. As we pass through villages, the locals line the roadside to wave and cheer. When we pull up for refreshments they swarm, pushing and jostling to touch us, hordes of cheeky little kids asking the same favours as the ones back in Delhi, as if they've somehow leap-frogged ahead of us. It's awful to say, but in the heat and dust the pestering becomes almost unbearable. I dream of a giant hosepipe to wash them away and cool myself down.

The skinny MD of the bus company has done all the driving so far. He has a co-driver but they don't appear to be getting on, perhaps because the co-driver seems more interested in the girl he has in tow rather than driving the bus.

Just across the Pakistan border, we pull over to the side of the road for yet another loo stop. An old Red Cross truck full of hippies heading for India has also stopped.

Our driver has a chat with their driver and returns with an announcement: "I've just been told some terrible news."

Everyone looks worried. I wonder if the bus has been busted for drugs, and we're all about to be thrown in some ancient Pakistan jail. It wouldn't surprise me in the least as the back-seat hippies have been sniffing, smoking, even surreptitiously injecting all the way so far.

"Hendrix is dead – found the other morning in his London flat. His German girlfriend has something to do with it."

All hell breaks loose. The co-driver's girlfriend is German. She starts screaming at the driver. "So, you are accusing the Germans of having killed Jimi? Fuck you! I know you hate us, but this is too much. I'm off."

The co-driver joins in. "Yeah, I'm off too. You can fucking drive this fucking bone-shaker back home yourself."

They grab their bags and jump off. The driver puts on his sunglasses, starts the engine and heads off as if nothing has happened. Alf taps me on the shoulder, and states the obvious.

"That lad can't drive solo all the way back to Blighty!"

However, our one and only driver turns on the bus's shaky sound system as loud as he can: *Purple Haze, Hey Joe, All Along the Watchtower.*

We sing along, except for Alf who has never heard of Jimi Hendrix.

Lahore is expensive and filthy and humid.

It's my first night under the stars. We've pulled into a hotel, but most of us kip in our sleeping bags beside the bus. Mosquitoes dive bomb us incessantly. I hardly sleep and feel like shit in the morning. Alf brews up some tea on his camping stove before we leave and that helps rouse me. He's seriously worried about only having one driver. Being ex-army he has an HGV license and is prepared to take over if necessary. I'm pleased to know that the driver took a room in the hotel. I'm also pleased we have Alf on board. I think he'll come in pretty handy as we wend our way west.

We enter the Khyber Pass in the early afternoon. The narrowness of the road with a sheer drop into oblivion on one side and threatening gunmetal grey mountains to the other side, all occasionally dotted with small fortress turrets, make for a death-defying drive.

Before long, we run out of petrol. The fuel gauge is evidently on the blink, and petrol stations have not been filling the tank to full despite charging for it. Of course, we run out of fuel on a precipitous edge where a strong gust of wind or the scrape of a bull-horned lorry could push us over the edge, tumbling hundreds of feet into the ravine.

Quite a traffic jam of lorries builds up, each one taking it in turn to cautiously squeeze past while trying not to knock us over the edge. Meanwhile our driver has hitchhiked off to the nearest petrol station.

Three hours later we are back on the road, singing along to *The Long and Winding Road.* With darkness falling we stop for the night at the Afghan border, again at a hotel that only the driver can afford.

Some sleep on the bus. I go with a dozen or so others to sleep on the roof of a half-built office block. We are woken at dawn by torrential rain and race back to the shelter of the bus. The driver turns up at 7am for an early start. We are all present and correct, looking forward to entering Afghanistan.

However, a problem emerges. We are parked off the road on a grass verge, which is by now a watery quagmire. The wheels spin in the mud not moving forward an inch. We are told to get off and push, which we all do except for the Danish hippies who refuse. Alf oversees the operation as if it were a military exercise. Everyone gets showered in mud, and still it pisses with rain.

This 'aint fun! The bus won't budge so our driver goes off in search of a friendly farmer and his tractor. Three hours later, one arrives and tows us off. Our sing-along changes to *Let it Be*.

Kabul

Alf is understandably more concerned than ever about having only one driver. He's offered to help but has been told he's not insured, which is probably correct. We've got thousands of miles ahead of us; quite a challenge for one slight guy who looks as if he'd be more comfortable driving a milk float.

The entry into Kabul is through a spectacular gorge amid mountains with turquoise lakes and rivers. I'm reminded of Switzerland. I wish I was in Switzerland with fresh, clean air, green fields, milk chocolate galore, golden-coloured beer and golden-haired girls with plaits, who can yodel and blow a mean Alpine horn…stop it! I'm hallucinating after only a few days in the Magic Bus. I blame the seats, which are seriously uncomfortable and lost their spring many centuries ago. My seatmate seems oblivious to everything, hardly uttering a word. I think she's turning into Frodo. On the other hand, Alf is driving me crazy, constantly tapping me on the shoulder and giving another lecture on the Raj and how to handle Wogs ("Workers On Government Service", as he's quick to point out.)

I like Kabul. It has an air of the wild west about it: horsemen galloping about in tribal robes with rifles slung over their backs; dodgy-looking bars with even dodgier-looking clientele polishing Kalashnikovs while quaffing the local brew; every male worth his salt seems to have a Desperate Dan beard. Without doubt this is a male-dominated town. Women are kept indoors. Market stalls don't sell fruit and veg, they sell guns – ancient and modern. And what looks like medieval instruments of torture – souvenirs to take home and hang on the sitting room wall.

I buy a white Afghan coat with black fur and embroidery. It's partly to keep me warm at night (sweltering during the day) and mostly to pose in on the King's Road when I get home. The problem is that the Afghan coat hasn't been cured, so it reeks. I also traded in my Dunlop golf bag for a grand leather grip to a stall-holder who wanted only a few dollars more.

The nice thing is it's not like a permanent rush hour here with crowds hassling you to buy stuff wherever you go. Sure, there are great drug bargains to be had for those so inclined. All you have to do is ask.

The transport is having a service, which hopefully will include mending the faulty fuel gauge. We plan to be here for a couple of days. I check into an inexpensive guesthouse, sharing a room with two other guys – undergraduates – from the coach.

The beds are the usual bunk-style wooden frames with crossed-rope to stretch our sleeping bags on. A small shady terrace offers good views of the distant mountains. I like to sit in the midday sun drinking sweet tea, occasionally thinking of the Golden Sheaf in Double Bay wondering if they still do a good brain sandwich.

Three Aussies in the guesthouse are heading home in a WWII Willys jeep. They say the worst is yet to come, particularly the desert trail. We'll evidently need all our reserves, let alone reliable transport.

The Desert of Death

From Kabul we head due south to Kandahar and then north again to Herat across what is known as "The Desert of Death". We are travelling at night, as it's too hot during the day. It's also bandit country, so there's to be no sleeping or lingering outside the bus.

Alf has shown me his starting pistol. "Just let one of them wogs start something, he'll have the Webley blasting his mush."

I'm reminded of the crazy model girl after the Mini Moke photo shoot. I suppose this Magic Bus lark is all getting a bit Russian Roulette.

We stop at an empty Russian-built hotel, midway into The Desert of Death. The place is quite bizarre: monolithic with a black marble lobby and courteous Russian staff who speak excellent English.

It feels like the set of a James Bond movie. Some people take rooms for a few hours' sleep before we head off again at dusk. I don't want to spend the money so choose to sit by the putrid green pool, so murky you can't see the bottom.

An athletic-looking pool boy is attempting to clean the sides with a long-handled broom. He has short-cropped fair hair and a muscled physique.

"He's military." Alf whispers in my ear, looking shiftily at the layout of the pool area and the well-kept gardens. "You can tell a mile away by the way he carries himself. So are the rest of them, right down to that tasty receptionist."

The temperature is well over 110F, too hot for sun bathing. I have a swim, as do a few others, but it is like a hot bath, and I'm afraid of swallowing water and catching something.

Alf and I go inside to the cool of the lobby area. Through a giant tinted glass window I see a Bedouin camel train on the near horizon, slowly moving across the barren desert in shimmering heat. I can't imagine what it must be like riding a camel through the furnace outside. There's nobody in the lobby. The reception desk is empty, the tasty blonde having done her business by checking a few weary travellers into rooms.

"She's probably a Red Army lieutenant from Moscow." Alf says. "Come on, let's do a little spying."

He leads me over to the registration book, which lies closed on her desk. Alf looks around to make sure nobody is looking and opens it. As expected, the names of our group appear on the first page. He flicks back a few pages.

"Blimey! Look at this lot."

About a dozen Russians, all high-ranking army.

Suddenly I'm aware of somebody standing behind us. It's the receptionist in her tailored outfit, thick stockings and sensible shoes. Not the best kit to wear in this heat.

"Can I help you?" She says.

Quick as a flash Alf replies, "I reckon my aunt Agatha stayed here a few weeks ago. She sent me a post card. I was just checking."

The receptionist snatches back the registration book. "You are mistaken." She barks. "Nobody of that name has ever stayed here. This is a luxury hotel."

At about 4am our reliable coach comes to a shuddering halt. It's pitch black outside. All we can hear is the distant howling of wolves. It appears the fuel gauge wasn't fixed properly. Of course it would be too much to hope for a spare tank of petrol on board.

Our driver says he'll hitch a lift to the nearest petrol station, a heroic statement in the middle of "The Desert of Death".

Some of the girls on board start to cry, wondering if the bandits or wolves will get him before anyone finds us.

My seatmate starts mumbling about a magic ring.

Alf gets out his Webley starting pistol and stands guard at the door to our four-wheeled casket. The hippies shoot-up and light up.

A rather intense young undergraduate from Cambridge University begins to sing a hymn: *For those in peril on the sea.*

I don't think one was written about the sand.

Surprisingly our foolishly fearless driver returns in less than an hour. By unbelievable good luck we have stopped just a few miles short of the only petrol depot for hundreds of miles. He was able to walk there with the jerry can and got a lift back in a lorry heading for Kandahar.

Now we have a new problem: the engine won't start. All of us step off, except the hippies of course, and push. Here we are in some godforsaken desert bump-starting a 1950s Leyland coach with wolves about to attack. And it's perishing cold. And there's a strong wind blowing sand all over us. And we are all knackered, it being dawn and nobody having slept properly for god knows how long. This really is fun! If my smart ad man pals could only see me now.

Alf cheers us up by explaining in great detail how the ignition has gone and won't be replaced until Tehran, days if not weeks away. It doesn't take a genius to work out that we'll be bump-starting until then.

Herat is a pleasant, sleepy kind of place with pine trees lining wide dusty avenues and a sandstone castle on a peak overlooking the town. It could be a Spa town in England, Leamington for instance, only a quarter of the size.

I'm in a spacious high-ceilinged room, shared with four others. A large ceiling fan slowly rotates to give some air to the otherwise sultry atmosphere. We are only staying one night before pushing on to the Iran border. Everyone keeps saying that can be a particularly tricky border post.

Tehran

A few miles short of the border we pull over to the side of the road. The driver switches off the engine.

"Now listen carefully, this is serious," he says, addressing the whole coach from the front of the aisle. "If we get searched and any, and I mean any, drugs whatsoever are found then we're all done for – probably in jail for years, with yours-truly quite likely facing the death penalty. So I'm giving you ten minutes to get rid of your gear. Okay? Got it? Ten minutes and I'm not fucking joking. Anyone who disobeys is dumped right here."

As if to lead from the front he gets off the bus, rolls a giant joint, lights it and casually puffs away as if it were a Hamlet cigar. I expect to hear Jacques Loussier playing Bach at any moment!

A number of others also get off and dig into their rucksacks, pulling out hidden vices as if they were girlie magazines. Joints are rolled and passed around; weed is scattered on the ground; pills are swallowed with any spare thrown away; powder is gulped down like lemon sherbet; pot is warmed by a match; Alf has got his camping stove out and is brewing a pot of "char". Most of this druggie action is coming from our hippy pals. The rest of the bus is reasonably clean, except for a bit of marijuana in a pocket or two.

However, the Danish hippy woman with purple hair occupying the back seat is in a furious argument with her hippy mates, who appear to be trying to reason with her. She's swearing, spitting, cursing like a witch in guttural Danish. After a few minutes of this tirade one of the hippies comes over to the driver. We all move closer to understand what the hell is going on. As usual the midday sun beats relentlessly giving the scrubland on either side of the road a combustible tinge.

"She refuses," he says. "She insists it not necessary for her. She has a doctor's note. The problem is she's a heroin addict, a true junkie."

There's no question about it. The addict with the purple hair is left on the roadside with her bags. She's waves her fists and curses like one of the witches in *Macbeth* as we bump-start the bus to get the hell away as quickly as possible.

One of the other hippies seems concerned, frightened even. "You may joke but she practises witchcraft. She'll put a curse on us, for sure."

We reach the border with Iran. I don't think I'm alone in feeling a touch queasy, that innate feeling of guilt when passing through customs with more than your duty free allowance. There's nothing to worry about, we're clean, but even Alf has gone quiet, which is unusual. It's a cauldron outside and the border guards look ominously official in their pale khaki outfits with rifles casually slung over a shoulder. As usual at border stops, the driver collects all our passports for inspection. A border guard takes them and then orders the driver to park in a security compound.

Two angry guards with trimmed black moustaches order us off the bus at gunpoint. There's an eerie kind of silence as we troop off: the quiet still of rank fear.

The mild-mannered Cambridge undergraduate asks if he can visit the lavatory, and he's clipped around the head with a rifle butt. He falls to the floor and wets himself. A guard kicks him and drags him up.

We are lined up against the side of the bus, thirty-one of us including the driver, who makes a desperate attempt to reason with the guards. He's told to shut up. Four guards aim rifles at us.

"It's a fucking firing squad." The Danish hippy yells.

Some of our group are hugging each other to stifle the crying. The Cambridge undergraduate who sang the hymn begins to recite *The Lord's Prayer*.

I'm numb. Beyond fear.

Alf is beside me. "Look 'em in the eyes," he whispers. "They're just bullying bastards. Don't let them feel the fear."

A commander appears from a small hut with a corrugated iron roof. He asks the driver if we are carrying drugs but doesn't accept the answer. "Search the bus and all the luggage." He commands his bullyboy guards.

For two hours we are held at gun point, in the blistering heat. A few have fainted and are allowed to be revived with water. Some have to visit the loo, but only with an armed guard watching. Most of the girls don't go for this option.

Mercifully, we are eventually cleared to carry on. We learn that the witch got a message through to say we were carrying drugs. It was true: she put a curse on us.

Alf has collapsed with chronic stomach pains. We are in the middle of nowhere. He thinks it's his ulcer and he may need hospital treatment – easier said than done. We lay him out on a double seat and give him the medicine he carries for such emergencies. This seems to do the trick and he dozes – or as much as anyone can with the bus bouncing around on a dirt track full of potholes.

The inevitable has also happened: the bus has broken down and Alf is the only one on board who knows anything about engines, and he's out of it.

Yet again luck seems to be on our side. A coachload of Aussies heading home pass by. They are with the Sundowners Company and have a mechanic who knows a thing or two about engines.

"You think you've got a problem mate? Our rear wheels have fallen off twice! The track ahead is pretty bloody rough."

Three hours later and we're on the road again.

It's midnight and we've reached Mashhad. We stop in preparation for a thirty-hour non-stop drive to Tehran. I'm pleased to see our one and only driver has checked into a cheap hotel, as has Alf, who seems much better now. I sleep on the coach with thirteen others.

Our marathon drive begins the next morning. Alf has moved to a spare seat next to the driver, "Just in case the silly bugger dozes off," he says. We all feel like cattle, losing all sense of feeling as we're transported through this alien land. Nobody talks, except Alf, who is on a mission to ear-bang the man in whose hands our destiny lies. My seat-mate spends most of the time curled up asleep; I think she's finally morphed into a Hobbit. Even the sound system has packed up, too exhausted to churn-out sing-a-long Beatles melodies any more.

The dust is dense inside the coach, so much so that I can no longer see the driver. I've tied a handkerchief around my nose and mouth in the style of a cowboy bandit, but it doesn't help. Everyone coughs and splutters. Any suspension the bus may have had is wrecked, as we've bounced at 20mph on a goat track full of craters – mere potholes are long since gone. We've broken down twice, the last time causing a huge traffic jam with Iranian lorry drivers threatening us as their eyes bulged with anger. We still have to bump-start the bus, and the gang of those strong enough to do so is getting smaller and smaller.

Eventually we cruise along a reasonable stretch of road, farmland on either side. Not far ahead is a herd of skinny goats, a farmer tending them at the side of the road. As we are just about to pass one of the goats bolts and races off in front of the bus. There's a sickening thud and a high-pitched bleat. The driver slams on the breaks and we all lurch forward, gear falling over us from the luggage racks. Within seconds the farmer is hammering on the cabin door, brandishing an antique rifle. Alf opens up, his starting pistol secreted behind his back.

From a garbled, crazed outburst, Alf interprets, saying we've killed the farmer's prize goat. Our driver produces a $10 note. The farmer goes bananas and aims the rifle at the driver who casually produces another $10 and passes it to Alf, who drops both notes on the ground in front of the farmer.

"Sorry about the goat." He says.

What should then have happened is that we drive off in a cloud of dust. But no, we have the indignity of a bump-start, with the shepherd laughing his head off.

We stop occasionally at a roadside store to stock up on basics such as fruit and water. The locals always help us with the bump-start. I think they quite enjoy pushing a dirty old coach full of young deadbeats and hippies. It's not the kind of thing they do every day.

The driving time feels stretched but it's because we are averaging only 30mph, or less. At least the tyres are holding out.

By nightfall we are thankfully on a main road speeding towards Tehran. Everyone is asleep, utterly exhausted. I can even see Alf has slumped over. Yet someone is staying awake, driving the bus at full speed. If he nods off then we are all done for. Dawn breaks on the outskirts of Tehran. We plan to stay three nights here while the bus has an extensive service.

I check into a hostel with most of the other passengers and share a room with three Cockney lads in their mid-twenties, who have very much kept to themselves. They immediately establish tribal credentials: they are militant West Ham football supporters and I'm a Chelsea fan.

After a good deal of taunting, they're prepared to forgive me. "Fancy a beer?" One of them suggests.

Apart from one night in Delhi with the goddess, not a drop has passed my lips. I'm gasping at the thought. We wander into the bazaar area and sit outside a small bar in a side street.

The Cockney lads have all been working in Melbourne for two years: one plumber, two painter-decorators. They couldn't stand Australia or Aussies and got "well pissed off" with all the pom bashing. They wanted a bit of an adventure together so chose the overland route.

"The trouble with Australia is it's got no bleedin' culture. I mean they've never even heard of Bobby Moore!"

The beer tastes like nectar and goes straight to our heads. "Are you as pissed off with this lark as we are?" They ask.

"Tell you what, why don't we fly home?"

I explain that I can't afford it.

"Nah, you've got the wrong idea. Typical Chelsea supporter! Follow us, sunshine."

We head off into the huge covered bazaar with them singing *I'm Forever Blowing Bubbles.* We may as well have entered Aladdin's Cave such is the massive array of trinkets and brass lamps and antiques on display. They head into the first shop they find with a large selection of rugs and carpets.

"Hello squire. We'd like to see some of your finest carpets if that's okay with you."

The enthusiastic storekeeper unrolls beautiful Persian rugs, giving a brief overview of their design and history.

One of the cockney lads sits on one of them and asks, "So how do I get it to take off?"

The store holder looks bemused. The cockney starts flapping his arms. "If it don't fly, what's the bleedin' point?"

Istanbul

When we arrive at Tehran's international airport, there's a great deal of excitement as some wag suggests that PBK Tours is going to foot the bill to fly us back to England.

In fact we're lost. Like all sprawling metropolises, it's easy to take the wrong road out. Alf has shot off the bus to get directions to Tabriz and the distant call of Europe. After about five minutes he comes racing back like an enthusiastic scout leader, khaki shorts flapping in the breeze. We set off again with much groaning at not boarding a plane, and the cockney lads resurrecting the flying carpet gag.

There's a refreshed air of enthusiasm on board after our rest. It definitely feels as though we are homeward bound. Even the Leyland luxury coach seems to have a new kick in its engine, possibly even a *tiger in its tank* now the fuel gauge has been fixed.

As dawn breaks we are back in the mountains: beautiful picture postcard scenery.

Alf comes up to me from his front seat. "There's something bloody wrong here. We should be in desert not bloody mountains!"

Evidently the driver won't hear of it, insisting we are on the right road. I naively ask about a map.

"It seems as if he forgot to buy one in Tehran. Bloody daft if you ask me."

At early morning, we arrive at a small fishing village on the Caspian Sea. We stop for breakfast and to find out where we are. I'm not an expert but from the sound of it I'd say the local language is Russian.

We're about 300 miles off track – that's the long and short of it. We've gone due north instead of west, and rebellion is brewing. The only problem is there's nowhere to run. We are stuck on the charabanc equivalent of the classic comedy movie *Monsieur Hulot's Holiday* – except, we're not on holiday or in the mood for comedy. The hippies are planning to jump bus as soon as we reach Istanbul. I may well join them. Perhaps I'll wait until Greece and pop down to the isles to recover. Who knows, I may even bump into Kerry.

Our driver takes a rash decision: to drive cross-country and meet up with the highway to Tabriz. The bus clearly doesn't like this and has spluttered to a halt on a steep gradient just outside a fishing village. Now the handbrake has gone and we're rolling backwards out of control. We lurch to a halt accompanied by the snapping of timber. Within minutes we are surrounded by what could well be police. It seems as if we've severed a tree planted in honour of a mayor. While the coach has been saved from rolling backwards into the Caspian Sea we've committed a jailable offence. Once more a wad of US dollars is produced and we are let off with a stern warning – in Russian. The problem is, as well as a dented rear, our transport appears to have a major engine problem. The atmosphere inside the bus is tense and bitter, as bitter as the cold wind outside. I wrap my Afghan coat around me and think positive: I've never been to Russia before.

Once more it's superman Alf to the rescue. Somehow or other, he's managed to find a garage with what he calls the "best mechanic in the land", whichever land that may be. We abandon the bus in the freezing cold while it's towed to the garage.

A number of us walk along the shore of the steely grey Caspian Sea, wondering where we might sleep the night in this one horse village.

Natural Brit irony is beginning to come to a head, "Don't worry chaps, we've got the pleasures of the Black Sea next!" one of the undergraduates quips, as if he were on a geography trip.

Mercifully the mechanic gets us going again by dusk. Alf has also been briefed in whichever language they have in common, presumably the generic voice of mechanics, on how to fix it if we have another problem.

"Top man," says Alf. "I've invited him to stay if he's ever passing through Nottingham."

I'm not sure Alf will feel so kindly when we break down yet again, well after midnight in the middle of nowhere in freezing rain.

And so we trundle on. Dust, heat, cold, breakdowns, bump-starts, bouncing about on barren roads that look like the no-man's land of the Great War; a tank would have difficulty traversing some of these tracks. We've even had a landslide narrowly miss us. I have to applaud the driver, his stamina is beyond human. God knows what he's on. After the terrifying border incident, it hasn't been difficult for those wanting to restock their drug supply.

We eventually pass through the border into Turkey and view many biblical landmarks, such as Mt Ararat, along the way. Yet such is the exhaustion factor, they all appear the same, like flickering images of a silent movie.

By entering Turkey I can feel the draw of Europe. Hedonistic gremlins happily lurk in my fantasies, there again maybe it's just hallucination from exhaustion: a filthy roadside restaurant becomes Mario and Franco's Trattoria Terrazza; a tented tea house, the "Hall of Mirrors" pub; milk churns turn into barrels of Guinness; a crumbling ruin, The National Gallery in Trafalgar Square; nomadic tribesmen on horseback, the Household Cavalry parading up the Mall to Buckingham Palace. I really don't know, or care, how long I've been on the trail – four weeks, maybe five? I yearn for civilization as I used to know it, however superficial that may be to others. I sing a song to myself to keep things going; silly, but it just has to be *Jumping Jack Flash*.

Fifty miles to Istanbul, and the road is now tarmac, a lovely winding route along the Bosporus. A clear blue sky wafts above us with just the hint of a golden sunset to come. Our spirits are raised by the thought of crossing the Bosporus by ferry, the point where east meets west. A good night's sleep in a cheap hotel in what many consider the most exciting city in the world, end destination of the Orient Express, fictionalized in romance and adventure by the likes of Graham Greene and Ian Fleming.

As if our transport knew what we were thinking it chose to splutter to a halt, one last gesture of defiance. Surprise, surprise! We've run out of petrol. Luckily the road is wide so we don't cause a jam. Tantalizingly we can just make out the Byzantine domes of the Blue Mosque on the distant horizon – so near and yet still so far away.

Our dogged driver sets off with the jerry can to a garage we passed a mile or two back. It's time for one last rousing rendition of *Let it Be*, accompanied by a drugged-up Danish hippy on his sitar.

LONDON

Late November 1970

The windows of Turnbull & Asser, the bespoke shirt maker at the end of seriously smart Jermyn Street, never cease to take my breath away. I must look a strange sight to be eying such finery: bearded with long, matted hair, filthy jeans and my stinking Afghan coat wrapped tightly around me to ward off the cold.

The shirts are magnificent in their bold stripes and pastel shades. How I would love to own one. I carry on down Jermyn Street soaking up the luxurious ambiance of the bespoke and exclusive antiques. I feel I've made the right decision. I'm back where I belong having had a life-forming experience. I wouldn't exactly call it "spiritual" in the way George Harrison bangs on about all things Indian, more...well, exhausting.

I pass the finest cheese shop in the world, Paxton & Whitfield, with its Dickensian scrubbed wooden floors and huge wheels of Stilton and other English cheeses, and head into Duke of York Street - and there's the Red Lion, just where I left it.

I've got half-an-hour to spare and can just about afford a half of bitter. I go into the "Hall of Mirrors" and the memories flood back, past and near present.

I stayed three nights in Istanbul with a few visits to the famous Pudding Shop Café to check out the hippies; some were about to embark on the trail east with gear a touch too new, almost with Kensington Flea Market labels still attached. Others, on the way home, tell tales of the nirvana I never noticed, let alone found.

It was "adios" to hippydom, for I was off to the Greek islands for some R&R. And that's just what I did. After selling my blood in Athens to raise a bit of extra cash, I took a ferry to Corfu and hung out there for a week at a beach bar with some nice American girls who were "doing Europe", in every sense of the word. Then I caught a ferry to Brindisi, hitchhiking on to Rome in three straight lifts. At a cheap pensione near the railway station I got friendly with a Canadian guy who was studying History of Art in London. He became my tour guide for all the sights and galleries. He was so good I moved up to Florence with him, but gave Venice a miss. I wanted to get back to London and had just about enough money for the rail fare. I checked in with my old buddy Willy (of the Tyrolean hat) and have been given a sofa in the doss house of a flat I once shared. My parents are on a round the world cruise, planning evidently to surprise me in Sydney for Christmas. My few goods and chattels are also on the high seas, not due in Southampton for a few weeks.

All I have is the clothes I'm wearing.

"Excuse me sir, you can't come in here dressed like that. This is a respectable establishment, London's top advertising agency."

Nothing has changed since I've been away; the walnut panelled lift still has an efficient whir to it; the glass shelves in reception are full of well-known household products. I'm looking forward to seeing Antonia again, wondering if she'll recognize me or whether I'll have the same problem I had with the commissionaire in persuading him that I am in fact a past employee. But there's no sign of Antonia, or the other woman who looked like Dame Edith Sitwell. An attractive receptionist tells me that Antonia left the agency to live in Gloucestershire, and the other lady has retired to Brighton.

A girl who could have passed for a model collects me from the fifth floor and takes me to my appointment. Unlike the commissionaire neither the new receptionist, nor the good-looking secretary, have batted an eyelid at my appearance. I'm shown into the all-familiar office with Raj prints on the wall.

"Good Lord, man! Who let you in? Are you who I think you are, in which case what on earth's happened to you?"

The major is more puce in the face than ever. "I told you that you should never have gone to Australia. A frightful place!"

I calmly explain about the lack of a job when I arrived in Sydney.

"So how can I help you?" The major asks rather callously.

I politely yet purposefully ask for my job back, explaining that I'm actually on my uppers.

"I can see that. Have you walked back to England?" He gives me one of his glazed stares, followed by a bit of a pregnant silence.

"Well you're in luck. We've just won a substantial new account and I'm after three account men as soon as possible." Another accusatory stare followed by a grunt. "But you're not damn well walking in here looking like a third rate tramp again. Go off and smarten yourself up, man."

Reluctantly, the major advances me a couple of hundred pounds from my first pay packet, so I head to a hairdresser with a royal warrant, G O. Trumper, and have a wet shave, shampoo and haircut. Next, I pop next door to Simpson's of Piccadilly to sort out a suit, shoes and other essentials. And it's a stroll down to the end of Jermyn Street, to Turnbull & Asser for a shirt or two. To hell with it! I'm an ad man, not a hippy.

Acknowledgements

A few years ago, over lunch, a friend of my daughter said he wanted to work in advertising. He asked how I started in the business. Over a few glasses of wine I related my story. Still awake he kindly said, “You should write a book.” Thank you James Forbes.

Luckily I had kept letters and postcards sent from the hippy trail. The rest I remembered, despite what they say about the sixties. But it took time, and I give thanks to family and friends for their occasional words of encouragement while I was locked away trying to make sense of it all.

I am more than grateful to Charlotte Darwin and Bernard Sanders for introducing me to someone who offered to read my manuscript. And I cannot thank Yvonne Barlow at Bookline & Thinker enough for her suggestions, patience, editing and commitment to making my lunch conversation become a reality.

Peter Maddick eventually left advertising to work in marketing for De Beers. He lives in south west London and Mallorca with his wife and two cats.